Appalachian Trail Happiness

Michael "Rev" Kane

ISBN: 069283236X
ISBN-13: 978-0692832363

DEDICATION

This book is dedicated to all of you, all of you who are out there doing everything to make this life amazing and I can't wait to meet you.

GRATITUDE

There are so many people who in one way or another made this an amazing experience. I've mentioned a lot of them in the book, from my first hiking partner Jim Cooper, to the person I spent the most time with on the trail Second Star, to my last hiking partner a really amazing woman from Scotland, my trail family was fantastic and I'll be forever grateful for my time with them. To the overall trail community, the hostel, B&B and hotel managers and owners, the trail angels, thank you for everything you're the best of us.

My family, blood and selected, who sent boxes, came to visit me on the trail, gave me rides and put me up in their homes when I was injured thank you. To all of those folks who followed along online and sent me messages of encouragement, thank you for your support it meant a lot. Also, to all the trail volunteers, the ATC and the regional clubs thank you for all you do to keep the trail such a wonderful resource for all of us.

In addition to everyone involved in the hike itself, there were people who really helped with the book. First and foremost, to one of my oldest friends who edited this text, John Thorne, thank you for the work and for over 40 years of friendship. I had a number of initial readers who gave me notes, thank you all, your feedback was invaluable in making this a better book. Finally a special thanks to my buddy Laura Ten Pas for her story about the Jersey Boys.

Preface

This book follows a certain flow: preface, introduction, journal entries interspersed with stories and explanations of the jargon hikers use on the Appalachian Trail. Finally, at the end, there are some reflections on life, the universe and everything. I'll talk about this more below, but wanted to set expectations right up-front.

I want to talk about what this book is and isn't. Let's start with what it isn't. This book is not a guide to thru-hiking the Appalachian Trail (AT); honestly I'm not sure any book is, but some certainly make aspirations in that direction. This one will not. This book isn't a travelogue; it will not detail my experiences from point-A to point-B on the trail. The book will have a certain chronological and geographic flow to it since I am using the writings I did on the trail and it made sense to include them (somewhat) in that order.

However, from time to time, like my hike, the story may jump around a bit. If you want to read a great travelogue about thru-hiking the AT, check out AWOL on the Appalachian Trail by David Miller; it's a book I love and highly recommend. It will give you a good sense of what the whole six-month thru-hike experience is like. Also, the author's AT guide has become the go-to guide book for thru-hikers; I used it, I recommend it, and, hell, as far as the AT is concerned, I wouldn't leave home without it. Not to mention, I've gotten to know David a bit and he's a great guy. Buy his books.

What this book is, is a collection of stories, recollections, and general writings from my time on the Appalachian Trail in the summer of 2015. I am not a thru-hiker; it was a potential goal, but my primary focus was to enjoy the journey, hike as far as my body and the fates would take me, enjoy the experience and get enough material for this book. Mission accomplished.

To have completed a thru-hike would have been magnificent icing on the cake, but a knee injury that never really healed would end that goal. This trip was the primary celebration I undertook for reaching the age of fifty and, honestly, if I had the chance, I would do it all over again.

What I hope you can get out of this book is a feeling for the Appalachian Trail Community: thru-hikers, hostel owners, trail towns and trail angels who all conspire to make hiking the AT an amazing experience. I knew the community existed, but the positive impact it had on me—the power of this community—completely caught me by surprise, a really pleasant surprise. Sure, there will be a good bit about the trail, the geography, the weather and the mountains, but it's mostly about the people, the culture and my own twisted brain. The book, as you will soon see, is drawn out of three things: my journal entries, descriptions and definitions of trail terms, and the writings I undertook while hiking the trail.

Finally, you will notice a heavy focus on and use of the word, happiness. This should not be a surprise given the title and the fact that I write a blog called the Ministry of Happiness (https://revkane.com). I'm a strong believer in aspiring to live a happy life, I also really strongly support the idea that experience, adventure, and stretching yourself are the best ways to get there. If you are not happy, then to become happy, or happier, you have to make changes—and change only occurs through action.

Hiking the Appalachian Trail certainly made me happy; I've seen a statistic that says 90% of thru-hikers report being happy 90% of the time. I have no idea what that number was based on or if it's real. I will tell you that assessment matched my observations on the trail. All-in-all, thru-hikers are generally a happy group, and hiking the Appalachian Trail led to many happy days for me and my friends.

So enjoy the book, drop me a line (Happinesskane@aol.com) and let me know what you think about it, and stop by the Ministry of Happiness (https://RevKane.com) and see what we're up to these days.

Michael "Rev" Kane

Introduction

In December of 2014 I had quit my job, sold my house and embarked on a journey to become happier. That journey would include hiking the roughly 2200 miles of the Appalachian Trail. I started my cross-country trip by staying for a few weeks at one of my favorite places, Anza Borrego State park in the Mojave Desert. One of the things I love about being in the desert is the impact it has on my mind; the desert makes me contemplative. Perhaps it's the openness of the environment or maybe the harshness. This contemplative state occurs for me even though desert camping drives a high level of focus on everything: from the highly variable weather, to the need to drink a lot of water, to the dangerous critters that abound. I find it to be a calming environment for me; my mind wanders and drifts to deeper-than-normal thoughts when I'm out there.

This particular trip also found me decompressing from my old life and transitioning into a period of travel and long-distance walking. This also led to a little more contemplation than normal. So, of course, to add to this state of mind, I read two books: Paulo Coehlo's The Alchemist, and Viktor Frankl's Man's Search for Meaning—two well-reviewed and excellent books that I've known about for a long time, have owned for some time, but had never read.

My focus in reading them will surprise no one, it was to delve even deeper into the idea of what happiness is and what really makes people happy. I had a number of thoughts while reading these books and the first revelation was a bit disconcerting.

People will more readily believe a fantasy about their life, rather than deal with its reality.

I see this all of the time, but the place I see it most often (and where it is most appropriate to me at this time) is the fantasy that people will pursue their dreams when they retire. Let me use the example of thru-hiking the Appalachian Trail, something many people have this on their bucket list. Many people plan to do it, but life gets in the way: jobs and kids come along, and the myriad day-to-day responsibilities we have prevent many of us from setting out to hike the trail. So we decide to wait until retirement.

But thru-hiking the AT is a grueling physical task; how many of us who retire at 60 (if we're lucky) or 65 (more likely) are still physically able to embark upon a six-month, 2200 mile hike? There are some—some really amazing folks—that are still physically able, but most of us are not at our peak physical condition at that age. Too many people put things off until later and then they never happen. This is one of the reasons I attempted this at 50 instead of waiting for retirement.

The second big revelation that I gained from these two books was a confirmation of something I think we all know:

Having a purpose gives life meaning, makes you happy and keeps you alive.

What I learned from reading Viktor E. Frankl's book was that the idea of meaning and purpose in life does not have to be grandiose. If someone can find hope, purpose—hell, even beauty—in the midst of a Nazi concentration camp, then it can't be that hard to find it in everyday life. Frankl talks about the biggies that give us purpose: children, love—basically, responsibility to others. But he demonstrates, through the most brutal of circumstances, what man is capable of being. He was able to find beauty in a sunset or the light coming through the forest. He found a way to laugh even when he knew that he was likely days from the gas chamber, and didn't know if his family was alive or dead. There is a post I wrote for the Ministry of Happiness called, Remember the Sweet Things; it is also a story from a Holocaust survivor about how just the smell of an orange can be a reason for joy and hope in your life.

Your purpose in life doesn't need to be creating world peace, becoming wealthy, famous, or becoming the President of the United States. Your purpose can be being a good parent, a kind person, someone who appreciates life. It comes back to something we hear time-and-time again, it is not our circumstances that determine our happiness, it is the decision we make, our response to these circumstances. Frankl said it much more poetically:

> "Everything can be taken from a man or woman but one thing: the last of human freedoms, to choose one's attitude in any set of circumstances to choose one's way."

My focus when I first wrote these words in December, 2014—my why—was to achieve my goal, to hike the Appalachian Trail for as long as I could, for as far as I could get. The big goal, the grand achievement, would have been to complete all 2200 miles; but the oil on the spoon, the immediacy of the journey (in terms Paolo Coehlo uses) was to enjoy each day out there and appreciate the freedom I'd created for myself. Spoiler alert, I didn't get the 2200 miles. But I got to do 1002 magnificent miles on the Appalachian Trail over what was a fantastic magnificent six-month experience.

As I traveled east, I was in the mood for mountains and hiking and camping, but there wasn't any place I was excited about exploring until I got to Arkansas. I considered a stay in Hot Springs, AR, but the weather was getting worse and so I mapped out a fairly direct route to Knoxville, Tennessee. My old college town was a place I expected to stay for a couple of days, catch up with some dear friends and perhaps take a hike in the Great Smoky Mountains out to the AT to maybe walk a few white blazes (the AT is marked by white blazes on the trail). From there I would head east and drive parallel to the AT, stopping in some trail towns and doing a little bit of hiking on the trail as both a shake-down and a teaser for my journey, before arriving in NY in late January. At least that was the plan.

However, as I got to Albuquerque, NM, my sister informed me that my mom, who had gone into the hospital due to a sodium imbalance, was having some severe stomach pains, and the doctors were concerned. The next day, she would be taken in for stomach surgery for a lacerated ulcer. My sister, who had transformed herself into superwoman, was working full-time, taking care of 3 kids, and looking after my mother in the hospital. She deserved help. So I put the pedal to the metal and hustled across a large chunk of the US in about two-and-a-half days.

I did have the good fortune of stopping in Knoxville and spending three glorious hours with the woman who is likely the love-of-my-life, and equally likely someone I'll never be with. But we have an incredible and deep connection, and we quickly slip into conversation and a comfort level that other couples only have after years together. She's someone I could talk to non-stop for months, but also someone who I could sit quietly with for hours, with no need for words needed from either of us. I needed that night with her, that time, the emotional cushion it provided, as the reports coming from the hospital in New York were increasingly worse.

The stomach surgery went well, but my mother now also had pneumonia and was very weak. When I arrived at the hospital she was not in good shape and deteriorating. For the next two days I sat by her bed and watched my mother literally slipping away, physical and mentally. It was incredibly hard to look at her laying there; she was uncomfortable, terrified and physically didn't even resemble herself. After two days, the conversations I was having with the doctors and nurses led to a paperwork hunt. We needed her health proxy and power-of-attorney documents, as well as her will. My oldest sister and I had a difficult, late-night discussion about things that truly seemed inevitable; we discussed the hard decisions we expected to have to shortly make. For several days neither of us slept well, wondering if the phone would ring at night to tell us our mother was dead. It was equally hard on my brother, who was not in town and getting the information via phone. He'd been able to visit the day before I arrived and understood the nature of the situation. It was an incredibly hard time for all of us.

Then, the next morning, I came in to the hospital and my mother was sitting up in a chair! I attributed this to her being one-half Appalachian Hillbilly. Hillbilly blood may be the toughest substance on earth. Over the next four days we would ride a roller coaster of improvement and despair. She was tough though, fighting pneumonia and a C-Diff infection. It would take a couple of weeks but she would recover enough to move to a rehab facility. Four weeks later she would actually walk up the stairs to her own home with limited help. She would eventually recover fully.

Eight weeks in NY, however, had NOT been the plan. Now, the plan was to head for the trail in early March in order to start at Springer Mt. and walk to Maine giving me time to pop-off and visit some folks and finish by September 1st. It sounded both straight-forward and wholly fantastical. I knew things would be difficult on the trail, even more so now that I'd basically gone from being fit and ready, to having had spent weeks sitting on my ass.

I expected that there would be physically difficult and emotionally fragile moments where the plan would seem horribly lost, the trip ridiculous folly. Those thoughts would absolutely come to fruition. I had often joked that my grandmother, who grew up on the Ohio River on the KY/OH border and who qualifies as full-blown Appalachian Hillbilly stock, was damn near impossible to kill. My mother has 50% Hillbilly blood and it seems to have served her well; I hoped that the 25% I possess would see me through my own trials on the trail and in life as well. Unfortunately, it would turn out that my granny was not impervious to death; she passed away while I was writing this book at the age of 90. She lived an amazing life and I miss her dearly, her love was an ever shining light in my life.

I would spend a few weeks training in the gym and scrambling to test gear and make last-minute adjustments. Unfortunately, amazing amounts of snow also fell in NY during the time I was in there, so getting any hiking in was out of the question. Then it happened. It had to happen right? Sooner or later the immensity of the task, the massive list of details, the kernels of self-doubt, all had to align to result in a major fucking freak-out. When it happened, I was less than 30 days from my start date. While reviewing my gear it suddenly hit me that I had somehow completely and totally overlooked buying a new winter bag for my first month in the mountains. I had a 32-degree bag; I was going to go into the mountains, in early March, in a hammock, with a 32-degree bag! Apparently, I was angling to be the new poster-child for hypothermia-awareness month.

So, I went on a mad buying spree: grabbing last-minute items, burning up some REI gift cards, flooding Amazon with orders. Freaking-out about my start date, my decreasing fitness while staying with family, figuring out which train to take, where to stay in Atlanta while visiting my friend, how I'd get to Springer from Atlanta: Aaaaaahhhhhhh! It was enough to give you angina. But at the end of the day, my sister made oatmeal chocolate-chip cookies, my favorite. I was back under control and breathing. I'm sure most thru-hikers, or about-to-be thru-hikers, know, or are about to know, that moment. It's OK; let it wash over you and then let it pass. Taking on something of the immensity of hiking the AT is bound to freak you out at some point, as it did me.

I would board a train bound for Atlanta on March 6th to start my adventure, after visiting with a close friend in Atlanta. My Osprey Exos pack was stuffed to the edges, including my brand new zero-degree sleeping bag, which, of course, would end-up being too hot for me.

The Three Questions

What are the three questions? They are simple:

What was the most beautiful thing I saw (encountered) today?

What did I learn today?

What made me happy today?

These questions were created for a couple of purposes: First, I have always been frustrated by the fact that when I travel I fall behind in my journaling, and then end up trying to catch up and, as a result, often miss days during the trip. I wanted a way to capture each day in a way that would be easy to complete at the end of long days. It would also be a method that would be easy to catch up on if I missed a day.

The three questions fit that criteria but also served an additional purpose: by recording these positive thoughts at the end of the day they acted as a reminder, even on the really hard days, that good things were happening every day. And because I knew I would be answering these questions at the end of the day it made me think more about (and helped me focus on) the beautiful, happy things that I encountered. I changed the first question from the original, "beautiful thing I saw each day" to "the most beautiful thing I encountered." Sometimes the most beautiful thing was a sound, a smell or an act of kindness.

CONTENTS

CHAPTER ONE

On the Trail

I would start my thru-hike by staying in the lodge at Amicalola Falls State Park the first night. I did a quick hike down into the visitor center and registered as a thru-hiker. Of course, the hike was in the rain, an omen of what the weather would be like the first couple of weeks on the trail. It would have been a lovely little hike had I not gambled and left my rain gear in the room. The next morning I set out across the park to meet up with a friend at The Len Foote Hike Inn. It's a hiker hotel in the forest—a little rustic, but absolutely beautiful—that provides communal meals and even ready-packed lunches you can take with you. I elected to do just that, and they even wrote an encouraging message on the bag. The cook was a former thru-hiker and made me a lunch worthy of my first day on the Appalachian Trail. It was a great experience; the next morning my friend, Jim Cooper, would hike me into the turn towards the trail: all-in-all a wonderful way to start my journey.

While at the Hike Inn, I met a hiker who appeared ready to have the best thru-hike story ever. First, a little description of the Approach Trail, what some people have called the hardest seven miles on the AT. The trail starts with six-hundred-and-four stairs and has caused many a potential thru-hiker to abandon their thru-hike before mile zero. I don't really think these seven miles compares to some of the gnarly climbs on the trail, but the combined anxiety of starting out, carrying too much weight, and then all of those damn stairs can easily do-in somebody, both physically and mentally. At the Hike Inn, I was told about two hikers who had showed up the day before I did. They had never met in person; they had been online gaming friends from the age of ten or so. They met in Amicalola and hit the Approach Trail. One of the two started complaining immediately and by time they saw the sign for the break off-trail for the Hike Inn, they immediately took it. That night the one friend called it quits and hiked back out and home. I met the second hiker at the Hike Inn, he was really down-in-the-dumps and seemed like he had a cold, He said he wasn't feeling well but intended to hike out the next day. I offered to hike out with him, letting him know that, given I was old and fat,

I'd likely be a pretty slow hiking companion. He seemed encouraged and we planned to hike out together the next morning with my friend, Jim, after breakfast. When breakfast came the next morning, and he walked in, I knew instantly he wasn't coming. I didn't say anything, but finally he said, "I'm going to spend another day here." The folks at the Hike Inn were kind, and they set up a work-for-stay for him that day. My hope is that he hiked out to the AT a few days later, but our paths never crossed and I think likely he went home.

March 4th – My first day on the Appalachian Trail, pre-Springer Mountain, non-counting miles. I was hiking as what we call a NOBO, a Northern Bound thru-hiker as opposed to a Southern Bound or SOBO. The most beautiful thing that I saw was an absolutely Tolkeinesque spot on the trail. I came around a corner and then over a small rise and encountered a set of stone steps that were surrounded by bright green moss and ferns. It was like a small piece of Middle Earth in the fog. It brought about an amazing feeling of satisfaction and calm. I had been really nervous about carrying the weight I would need, and what I learned that day was that five miles on the Appalachian Trail with a forty-plus-pound pack was possible. What made me happy was just finally being on the trail, after months of preparation and thinking about it, after quitting my job, after traveling across the country and making my way to Georgia, I was finally doing it. I was also happy because my good friend, Jim Cooper, met me at the Len Foote, Hike Inn and hiked me in on my first day. All-in-all, a spectacular day!

That night was a jumble of emotions, my gear spread out across my little room at the Hike Inn. I was excited to be getting started, I was nervous about how I would do. I had a lot of hiking experience but had never tackled an unsupported hike at this level. I slept surprisingly well considering all the noise in my head.

March 5th – Springer Mountain; first actual countable miles on the trail. The most beautiful thing I saw was the summit of Springer Mountain, mile zero. The view was foggy and cold. I met my first thru-hikers on the summit and bumped into two trail angels I'd met at the Hike Inn. The day would turn from cold-and-foggy to cold-and-rainy. I hung out at Stover Creek Shelter near sunset trying to decide whether to sleep in there. Every time I started to leave, the rain kicked up harder. Finally, knowing I wouldn't sleep comfortably in the shelter, I decided to move on. I felt so out of place, so alien, at that moment—and so completely unconfident in my abilities. There were a number of folks in the shelter already buttoned-up in their bags, pre-sunset. It seemed that everyone knew so much more about this process than I did. The promise of bad sleep and feeling almost like I'd be intruding in the shelter made the decision to move on pretty easy, even in the rain. So I pushed on and set up my hammock in the forest, stealth camping on my first night at a place called Three Forks. The rain had changed to sleet as I set up, and what I learned was that even under completely terrible conditions, I could set up camp and stay warm. Of course, the changing conditions, and the fact that the temperature dropped to 18, meant that all of my knots had frozen. So I spent my very first morning digging my first cat hole and then blowing on all of the knots on the hammock to get them melted enough to untie.

Everything made me happy that day, the beauty of the first real day on the trail, the hard walking with too much weight, setting up in lousy weather, crawling into the hammock, even all of the noises I heard at night that I was sure were bears coming to eat me—every bit of it made me happy. I was finally on the Appalachian Trail!

March 6th – The most beautiful thing I saw on the trail were frosted trees. The early morning part of the trail was surreal and beautiful as the trees were coated like someone had spray-frosted them. I climbed Sassafras Mountain; it was a hard climb that I really enjoyed. I like climbs with a consistent slope, and even though the slope was fairly brutal it was consistent and that made for good climbing. What I learned was that as tough as things were, I was determined to move forward and make progress. This was driven home to me because several other folks I hiked with in the morning called it an early day, or took a lot of rest breaks. I felt really good about my effort and how well I was doing, even after sitting around for weeks. What made me happy were the views off Sassafras; the leaves weren't out yet and, as the sun came out, the views across the valley were spectacular. I also met two really interesting hikers. First, a SOBO who was on his last day and heading for Springer; he looked soooo damn happy. Then, as I hit the top of Sassafras, a big ole hiker, splayed out on a big flat rock, lying in the sun like someone's pet Labrador. Not sure I've ever seen anyone more relaxed and happy than he was in that moment.

March 7th – I was making my way to the Lance Creek campground; I expected it to be pretty full, as it was the back-end of a ten-mile run that required bear canisters if you stayed in that area. I was happy to make the campground in daylight, as opposed to arriving at night like I had the previous day. The campground was absolutely packed; I'd say thirty to forty folks as I came in, which meant walking pretty far into the campground to find a spot. The most beautiful thing I saw was, once again, the view off of the mountains. In that part of Georgia, prior to leaf-out, the views off of the side of the mountains are really spectacular. What I learned, unfortunately, was that I had an issue developing with the left strap on my pack; it would slowly slide out so that every hour or so I would have to readjust my pack. What made me happy was the simplest of things; as I entered the campground at Lance Creek, someone yelled, "Hey, Reverend." It was nice to feel the community forming and to start to feel a part of it. I was certainly hiking as part of the Bubble.

The Bubble is a very fluid term; it generally refers to the large grouping of hikers, all present on the trail at the same time. Some times of the year are more popular than others for the Bubble to form. In the spring, most NOBO's start between March first and April fifteenth; so that group, due to varying pace, ends up being a pulse of hikers that passes through areas over about a three-week period. Of course, this happens in reverse with SOBO's and, really, a bubble forms any time a big group of people start out around the same time. Your bubble becomes your extended community, familiar faces to see in towns and on the trail. You trade news, stories, and information about fellow hikers you have in common. It creates a wonderful sense of community. It is the reason I recommend folks start out in the spring and head north. Having that extended community makes every bit of the experience better. Sure, a little of the normal societal nonsense found in any human group creeps in, but, all-in-all, the bubble makes things better. This was really driven home for me on two occasions. The first was after I spent a week rehabbing my injured knee in Damascus and, as a result, ended up behind the bubble I'd started with. As I hiked through the Grayson Highlands, folks were noticeably less friendly and even suspicious of me. One person, after getting to know me a bit, told me she had wondered where the hell I came from. A perfectly idiotic question as there will always be folks who catch up to you; but where your bubble becomes "us," other hikers outside that community are sometimes viewed as "them." The other place this really resonated for me was after my second knee injury, when I was slackpacking south through MA. I would occasionally bump into solo NOBO's whom I knew, and their first question was, "Who's up ahead of me?" After spending time with the group, long days of solo hiking starts to wear most folks down mentally; it's amazing how invigorating a familiar, friendly face is on the trail.

March 8th - Lance Creek to Neels Gap and my first zero day! This, of course, meant climbing over Blood Mountain, the highest point on the Appalachian Trail in Georgia at 4461 feet. The day was absolutely gorgeous; I had a great day hiking with Backtrack, whom I'd recently met. I stopped for a snack and met Mad Hatter, Lizze and Quiet Waters for the first time. The climb up Blood Mountain contains a bunch of false summits. I had been tipped-off about this, and knowing it ahead of time was a good thing, as it kept my frustration levels down on the climb. It was a beautiful climb; the terrain went from standard hardwood forest to tightly-packed rhododendrons, which I kept thinking were great places for bears to hide. The shelter on top of Blood Mountain was really nice, there were a lot of thru- and day-hikers on top. I even met someone who'd done the same Himalayan hike I'd done five years prior. The most beautiful thing I saw that day were the views off the top of the mountain. The views coming up had been great over the last couple of days, but to be on top of Georgia was absolutely wonderful. The descent down (have I mentioned I'm a bad descender?) absolutely sucked. There were lots of boulder areas with sharp cuts, and it took what seemed like forever to come down that hill. What I learned that day was that I was a really solid ascender and an absolutely pitiful descender. The thing that made me happy that day happened while I was eating lunch. I was sitting on a boulder when a woman came flying up the trail with a guy in tow. She looked right at me and said, "What is your trail name?" She said it fairly forcefully and I was a little nervous about why she wanted to know, but I replied, "Reverend Kane." She immediately yelled, "I'm Janey from Twitter." We'd been talking for some time on Twitter and it was awesome to meet someone from Twitter in person. We gave each other a hug and took a couple of photos. We'd cross paths again a couple of times on the trail, and she's absolutely one of my favorite people from the trail. I'd meet a couple of other folks from Twitter as well over the course of my hike; it's amazing how social media has changed the trail experience.

A Trail Groupie Experience

Now, one of the things I'd written-off prior to starting my AT experience was the idea of romance at any level. Given that the majority of the hikers are twenty-five and under and the remaining are typically post retirement age, a fifty year-old guy doesn't expect romance on the AT. Sure, it could happen, and I'll admit to meeting a couple of women who were in the right age-range; if circumstances were different we might have taken the time to get to know each other better. But romance with the non-hiking public I thought would way off the table, considering I had the general appearance of a homeless serial killer who hadn't showered in many days. Of course, the world is an amazing and diverse place and one concept I had never considered actually exists: thru-hiking groupies.

Now, before anyone's imagination runs away, we're not talking rock star groupies. Although the image of a bunch of young girls hanging around the base of mountains waiting for thru-hikers to descend definitely raises a smile, that is not what I'm talking about. I encountered my first groupie on the descent off of Blood Mountain.

As I mentioned earlier, it had been a hard descent and I'm not much of a descender. So, after climbing down boulders for a time I finally hit a less rocky, somewhat normal trail. I was happy to finally be walking instead of scrambling, and I knew I was near the bottom. So I decided to take a break and have something to eat.

About this time a family came walking up the trail: parents in their 30's and a couple of younger kids. They were friendly and stopped to say hi and they asked if I was a thru-hiker. Well, to be accurate, the mom asked. When I said yes, she broke out a really wide smile and her dark brown eyes became intensely focused on me. She started asking a lot of questions and standing closer to me. Her husband announced they were moving on and they started heading up the mountain. Well, *they* did. *She* stayed another of couple of minutes, telling me how much she admired me and how wonderful it was what I was doing. She was very touchy while she talked to me, touching one strap, untwisting another. Her husband called her name at least three times before she finally moved on, but she made sure to wave on top of the next switchback when she caught my eye.

My first thought was, I've been out here too long already if I think married women are flirting with me this much in front of their husbands. Later that day, sitting around with Backtrack and the Mad Hatter, Backtrack said, "Did you see that good-looking brunette with her family?" I acknowledged I had and he instantly said, "She made me uncomfortable as hell; she was flirting with me right in front of her husband." I burst out laughing and relayed my own story, which got us wondering if there was such a thing as trail groupies. I would have two other very similar experiences on the trail and would hear from several other hikers about their own. It's a curious phenomenon that I can only chalk up to bored housewife syndrome (although, admittedly, my third encounter was with an unmarried couple). I think there is a population of women who love the idea of adventure and romanticize the idea of thru-hiking the AT. Encountering a thru-hiker excites them and they feel drawn. I'm not sure anything would ever happen between them and a hiker, but they definitely throw a boat-load of attention your way. To be completely honest, being on the trail, tired, dirty and smelly, it feels pretty damn good to get that attention.

March 9th – For my first zero day. I had originally planned to crash in the hostel at Neels Gap for the night and head out the next day. Another hiker had told me there were cabins next door and that really paid-off. When I got to Neels Gap, the hostel was almost full and the water wasn't working and that sealed it. I asked them to call down to the cabins for me and I reserved one for the night. The cabins were great, I damn near ate-out the camp store. It was wonderful; they had frozen pizzas and ice cream, which I made great use of that first night. A long, hot shower was another joy, as was a bed and cable TV. Backtrack and Mad Hatter were sharing a cabin there as well and so we spent some time hanging out at Mountains Crossing, eating, resupplying and sending home shit we didn't need. The most beautiful thing I saw that day was Backtrack re-gearing. He'd been carrying a huge pack of about sixty-plus pounds. He swapped-out packs and other gear and sent home a lot more. All-in-all, he shed fifteen pounds off of his pack weight that day. What I learned was a hiking technique Mad Hatter taught me. It is called the rest step and was made famous by Colin Fletcher. Once I figured out exactly what it was, I realized I was already doing a variation of it while climbing. What made me happy that day is an easy answer: rest, good friends and lots of food.

Meeting A Trail Legend

While at Mountain Crossing I overheard someone call this raggedy, gray-haired fellow, "Jack" and the name clicked in my head. I turned to him and asked, "Are you Baltimore Jack?" He smiled and said, yes, and I had a rude message for him that one of his hiking buddies had me asked me to pass along. He laughed and knew exactly who I was talking about. We would talk about hiking for about 15 minutes; it was a short and pleasant conversation. Jack had an easy laugh and was a bit of a wise-ass, but very kind. He told me we might cross paths later that year as he was thinking about hiking some of the Long Trail in Vermont. Unfortunately, Jack never got back on the trail, and earlier this year he passed away. He was an interesting character and if you hike the AT you will likely hear any number stories about him. I've heard a few, but won't add them here; they are best heard in a group of hikers at a shelter in the forest.

CHAPTER TWO

March 10th – A nice day after a good rest, we would do a little over ten miles this day. For the first time on the trail I had company the whole day, as Backtrack and I hiked together. As we came into camp, Backtrack mentioned that this was his first ever double-digit hiking day—a hell of a way and a hell of a place to start. At one point we were doing a fairly technical descent on slippery mud and rocks, and we hated it. I checked the map and determined that we had another 1500 feet to descend before we leveled out again. It was a totally depressing moment which soon led to the most beautiful thing I saw all day. After another few minutes descending I kept seeing something I couldn't quite identify; I kept walking and looking, stopping and looking, and finally it dawned on me what it was: a road. It was gorgeous damp tarmac with a double yellow line running down the middle. I'd misread the guide; it was a 150 foot, not a 1500 foot, descent. What I learned on the trail that day was that, as much of a loner as I am, and as much as I enjoy solo hiking, it's great to have good company on the trail. What made me happy during the day was my first official trail magic at one of the gaps. It was just snacks and drinks but was a completely uplifting and awesome experience.

Trail Angels & Trail Magic

I often talk about trail community. The community extends well beyond the folks who are actually on the trail hiking. It includes the towns along the trail, the hostel owners, the outfitters and, of course, the Trail Angels. Trail Angels are folks who help hikers by providing trail magic. I was more cynical of humanity when I went out on the trail than I am now. I have the kindness of trail angels to thank for that change in me. Trail angels offer trail magic in the form of free rides, free food, and, in some instances, even free places to stay. Plus they offer a vairiety of other small kindness that a hiker needs. They are truly angels; there isn't a better feeling than turning a corner on a hot day, seeing a cooler sitting next to the trail, and then opening the lid to find cold drinks and snacks inside. It's not just because you're hot and short on calories, but because of the kindness. Someone cares enough about you to make the effort to provide just what you need at that moment, someone who you will likely never meet and never be able to thank. So why do they do it?

In my experience from talking to various trail angels there are a lot of different reasons. Some are former hikers repaying the kindness they received on the trail. Some are folks who can't hike, but have a love for the trail and hikers and just want to be part of the community. Some feel it's their mission in life to be kind to others. Some are just nice, often lonely, people who use this way to have some social interaction. I didn't expect the kindness without strings; I figured the religious groups wanted to preach, or folks were looking for tips, or, possibly, there were other nefarious reasons the interactions. I'm sure those things have or will happen; but in my experience, trail angels are the salt of the earth, and their altruism has given me more faith in my fellow man.

During my time on the trail, I received all manners of cookies, cakes, chips, beer, soda, water, iced tea, lemonade, candy bars, cliff bars, hot dogs, spaghetti, sandwiches, and even a really spectacular grilled-cheese sandwich with bacon. That particular kindness was given to me at a trail angel camp. These folks come to the AT for a week and set up camp for one single purpose: to provide trail magic for hikers. These particular angels told me that even though they spend a week making food, giving out snacks and drinks, and providing a really comfortable and friendly place to take a break, they actually get more out of the experience than the hikers do. There is a satisfaction that comes from being incredibly kind and giving and these folks harvest this type of satisfaction by the bucket-load. Hiking the AT would not be the same experience without these wonderful human beings.

The Story of Backtrack

On a long-distance hike you meet a lot of really tough people on the trail. I knew a hiker who broke her arm and came back on the trail in a full cast and finished her hike. Someone who would become a good friend started, got appendicitis, returned six weeks later, and finished. I met folks suffering from PTSD and a range of other emotional life traumas who did the whole trail.

I also met so many kind people: hikers in camp who would give you food or fuel for your stove; folks who would hang back with you on the trail if you were having a bad day; some who shared food from boxes from home, rides from family members, free stays in hotel rooms, and free meals. And that doesn't include trail angels and hostel owners who gave of themselves numerous times.

But I met one hiker who has become a close friend and who was both tougher and kinder than all of them, his name was Backtrack. Backtrack is a big man, well over six-feet tall and north of two-hundred-and-fifty pounds. When I met him he was carrying a pack that weighed over sixty pounds. I liked him immediately; he has a calming and inviting personality. This is who he is. He's one of those rare people who is truly interested in every person he meets; when you speak with him you get his full, genuine attention. He's one of the most social people I've ever met. When we would enter camp at night he would need to talk with people before he did anything else. Because it was early in the spring, this often led to setting-up and cooking in the dark; but, to him, it was necessary—he needed that social contact. This trait made him and me unlikely friends, and even less likely hiking partners. But, like I said, I liked him immediately, and, even though we were on opposite ends of the social-need spectrum, we have a lot in common. We both are well-read and like to talk across multiple subjects. We're both pretty straight-forward folks. We both like sports, and it is rare to find someone who can intelligently talk about anything from Faulkner to football.

The first day we hiked together it actually crossed my mind that he might soon die on the trail. You see, Backtrack was not a hiker. I don't mean this in a derogatory way; he'd been an athlete in college and had been in the military for decades. He just had never really hiked before. When I set out on the Appalachian Trail I had never done a self-supported long-distance hike. But I had done short unsupported hikes and even a twenty-two day supported hike in the high passes of the Himalayas. Backtrack . . . well he'd seen some hiking on TV.

A change in life left the big man at a fork in the road and he made the type of decision I encourage people to do all of the time on the Ministry of Happiness Blog. He took a risk and decided to challenge and push himself. Of course, I usually advise a bit more planning. You see, about a month before embarking on a 2200 mile thru-hike on one of the toughest long-distance trails on earth, Backtrack dropped a credit card on the counter at his local REI and said, "Give me everything I need to hike the Appalachian Trail."

He did not go half-assed either. He bought cases of Mountain House foods, including several cases of the biscuits and gravy which, he would discover on the trail, he really didn't like. He bought cases of Cliff Bars, all manner of solid gear, and all of the state trail maps for the entire trail, (which, of course, he was carrying from day one). Having almost no backpacking experience, he lumbered as he walked under the weight of his pack. I was with him when we finished a ten-mile day, and he was so happy. I asked why. Turns out it was the first double-digit hiking day in his entire life.

Of course, he had never really learned how to properly pack a pack. His beautiful Scarpa full-leather Gortex hiking boots were fantastic, albeit horribly the wrong size. He had never learned how to pace himself on a climb, but he also was stubborn as hell and would not slow down; when he came up behind you on a hill, you thought you were being chased by a bear. Upon visual inspection, the grunting sounds were not ursine but of a man who appeared to be on the edge of a massive heart attack; he sweat like a sprinkler system.

But like I said, he was amazingly likeable, and the hikers he met were good and kind people. The Mad Hatter had hold of him first and helped him with his pack and gear. I got him next and taught him how to breathe and climb. At our first zero day at Neels Gap, he bought a new, much lighter pack and sent fifteen pounds of gear home. He's a natural athlete, and someone who pays attention and learns quickly. By the time we hit Franklin, NC, he was on par with my level of hiking skill. By the time we hit Hot Springs, NC, he was a better hiker than I was.

That's why it was such a catastrophe that his body betrayed him. You see, he has a defect in the structure of his knees. Under the weight and stress of day-to-day hiking, his knees degraded quickly. It hadn't helped that his first pair of shoes had literally sliced his feet to shreds. (And it would be that way until he got properly fitted in

Franklin.) So, put yourself in his shoes: no hiking skills, feet being shredded to pieces, knees and God-knows-what-else hurting, a two-hundred and fifty pound body, and a sixty-pound pack. Frankly, if that's me I'd be the biggest, whiniest bitch on two feet. He barely complained, never asked us to slow down, and was consistently in good spirits. Frankly, he might be the toughest and most positive son-of-a-bitch I've ever met. Under these conditions (although with better shoes and much more painful knees), he would hump, step-for-step, and sometimes out-hike a lot of us, up, down and over five-and six-thousand foot mountains. He's just plain amazing.

Our group was heartbroken when we left him behind in Erwin, TN. We'd stayed there to get him to an orthopedic doctor to get examined. The initial prognosis was three-to-four weeks of rest and rehab. Our plan was to meet him in Damascus where he'd be rehabbing his knees and where he'd rejoin us. We all had a sense, however, that the odds were not in his favor. When I arrived in Damascus he, was there, but more than just *there*. He'd moved into a hotel in Abingdon, and with nothing but rehab to do he had become Backtrack: the trail angel. He was slackpacking hikers, giving rides, occasionally letting broke hikers crash with him. He was basically being a cheerleader and support crew for AT hikers.

Reuniting with him in Damascus was great; our group had split-up by then and I would get to briefly overlap with Mad Hatter, Jedi and Second Star in Damascus. I spent a week there doing my own version of knee rehab. It had become obvious Backtrack would not be getting back on the trail. But he had a plan; he'd return to the west coast and come east in his RV and play support crew for the rest of us all the way through to Maine. People say things like this all of the time and never follow through. Six weeks later, Backtrack would arrive on the East Coast to pick up Jedi and slack pack him for a few days. He would end up doing that for all of us: pick us up in his jeep, take us back to the absolute luxury of hot showers, movies, air conditioning, hot meals and of course cold Coca-Colas. Some of you may have heard of the legendary trail angel, Miss Janet, who each year flows with the bubble doing much the same thing. Well, Backtrack was our own personal Miss Janet and support team. This is why I will always refer to him as the toughest and nicest guy I met on the AT, and I am happy to call him my friend.

March 11th – This was a prototypical early day on the Appalachian Trail. We hiked a little less than eight miles and it took us all day. What we encountered that day was my least favorite place on the AT, Blue Mountain. Not so much a mountain but a large rock-fall in the shape of a mountain. Climbing was no fun, and descents (even small ones) were an absolute horror, filled with slips, falls and rolled ankles. It meant for a long, tough, and utterly frustrating day; one of those rare days where hiking made me more stressed and uptight than I was before I hit the trail. We arrived late in the day and it was raining. I decided for the first time to sleep in a shelter. It would also be my first nearly sleepless night. I was using a small Thermarest air mattress that had not nearly enough cushion for my taste. The shelter was packed, and several times I made contact with the couple next to me. What's more, throughout the early evening, hikers showed up, lit up the shelter with their headlamps and made a ton of noise. I also had my first mouse encounter; I felt something crawling on my bag and flung it off me to hear something thud on the wall.

The only upside was that I got to pull my Bob shtick on one of the hikers; it was something I told Backtrack about it earlier in the day (and I'll describe it in a moment). The most beautiful thing I encountered that day was the sound of owls hunting at night as I lay there not sleeping. I was learning that I was going to need patience with my fellow hikers, especially in shelters which I now knew I would rarely use. What made me happy that day was seeing the shelter ahead of us, which signified the end-point of a very long day. Unfortunately, the day had really tanked my mood between the terrain of Blue Mountain. It had been a hard, long day with rain, and after a complete lack of sleep.

Bob the Trans-dimensional Being

So I have a pair of Black Diamond trekking poles that I've had for years. I bought them for my Himalayan hike. They're great, tough as hell, and have served me far longer than I would ever have imagined they would last. Well, I'm a bit of an asshole and I have to admit, I love screwing with people's heads—not maliciously or too deeply, but enough to have a bit of fun.

One way I do this is with Bob. You see, I refer to my right trekking pole as Bob. There is no real right or left to the poles, but I wrap some duct tape on my poles to carry it. I like having two-different widths available so I always wrap the thinner tape on Bob. So, every morning when I get up, I grab my poles and say, "Good morning Bob," to the right one. It's a set up, and I wait for that one person who will finally say to me, "Bob?" Yes, Bob, I reply, and that's when they inevitably bite and ask the name of the other pole. To which I reply, "It's a damn trekking pole, why the hell would you name a pole?" I then huff, shake my head, and walk away down the trail. This happened during my morning at Blue Mountain shelter.

One morning on the trail it happened—and happily with a hiker who I wasn't particularly fond of. I always hoped that the person catches up to me, confused, and wants to know why I call the other pole Bob. I then calmly explain that it's because Bob is not a trekking pole, but in fact a transdimensional being who is on our Earth to explore. Since he wanted to explore, he thought taking the form of a trekking pole would be a great way to see a lot of our world. I point out, of course, that it's really worked out well for him, given I'd taken him from the Himalayas to the Appalachian Mountains. "You see," I tell them, "I would have never known what he was, but I accidentally left him laying on some Peyote out in the desert and it caused him to hallucinate. In that state he telepathically blew his cover and told me all about himself. So, yeah, Bob." I then smile, turn, and walk away. It's always good if people think you're just a little bit nuts, and Bob agrees.

March 12th – Blue Mountain Shelter to Unicoi Gap. Rain again, the morning was a quick run down into the gap. Most folks don't stop at Unicoi, or at least don't go into Helen. It can be an early jump-off point to go into Hiawassee, but most people hike another couple of days before leaving the trail for town. However, I had heard about Helen, GA, the little faux German Alpine Village, when I attended the University of Tennessee, so I had thought I might check it out. By time I got to the gap, my third day in rain with little sleep and my mood tanking, the "maybe" became a "definite." I called a shuttle and got a quick ride into town. The most beautiful thing I saw that day occurred during the morning on the descent. For a couple of minutes the sun broke through the fog and it was really amazing. What I learned was something I had already known, my knees are not strong. They were a bit stiff and sore so that was another reason to pull off into Helen. What made me happy, a little thing, was that I found a little package of chocolate donuts in my food bag. I had forgotten I had them. There is nothing tastier for breakfast on a cold, wet and foggy morning in the mountains than tiny chocolate donuts.

How Big Daddy's Calamari Fingers Saved My Hike

By time I'd gotten to Helen, GA, I was in a truly foul mood. My first night in a shelter the night before had been fine, but I hadn't gotten any sleep. The couple sleeping next to me accidentally kicked me several times during the night. I had a mouse run up the front of my bag, and there also was the normal snoring and moving around on air mattresses. At one point, way past hiker midnight, some hikers arrived, ripped open the tarp and blasted us all with their headlamps. My Thermarest air mattress was not going to work for me; so, all-in-all, if I got an hour of sleep I don't remember it. I got up at dawn and headed for the gap. It was raining again; I think this was the fourth straight day of pretty consistent rain, and it would rain, snow or sleet for twelve of the first fourteen days I spent on the trail.

Happily, I was able to connect pretty quickly on a ride into Helen. Upon arrival at the hotel, I immediately noticed that they'd recently had a fire, as the entire breakfast area was hidden behind duct-taped plastic. It reeked of smoke. They gave me a coupon for breakfast at the Waffle House for the next morning, so I was fine. I headed for my room. My gear was soaked-through, and I hit my room, dropped my pack and popped on the TV. It was local weather with a goofy little man pointing at the weather map: "Rain today, rain tomorrow; it's gonna rain like heck! That's right, Rev, start building a damn ark—rain, rain, rain!" OK, maybe that's not an exact quote, but it's what I heard. I'd had enough damn rain; I immediately walked back to the front desk and booked a second night. That moment was the closest I got to quitting the trail for reasons other than injury. It was because of where my head was at.

Your mental state is every bit as important as your physical state when you are on the trail. At the beginning of the trail, you still don't know if you can be a thru-hiker; your body is still adapting. Typically, in the spring, in Georgia, the weather is cold and wet and the trail is muddy, rock-filled and slippery. You fall—I did, numerous times—and hopefully these falls only hurt your pride. So, early on you are at your most fragile. Then, after multiple days of rain, a little bit of pain and doubt, quitting is easy. It is said that thirty-percent of all the people who attempt a thru-hike on the Appalachian Trail quit within the first thirty miles. That day in Georgia I came to full understanding of why that happens.

So it was in this state of mind that I hung my gear all over the room. It looked like an eight-year-old's pillow fort on steroids. I showered and put on my town shorts and a damp shirt and went out to get some food. Right across from my room was Big Daddy's, which looked like every "get-a-burger-and-a-Bud" sports bar I'd ever seen in the southeast. And although I was sure it was filled with people who would give me funny looks and maybe even attitude, I didn't care. So I stomped across the pond that had formed between the hotel and the restaurant, my shoes and socks already soaked anyway, and I walked into Big Daddy's. On the menu, calamari fingers caught my attention. I have a thing about calamari; I love it, but only if its calamari steak that has been cut and deep-fried, otherwise the little rings and tentacles have a tendency to taste like breaded rubber to me. But the description for the calamari fingers seemed like something I'd I enjoy and so I ordered them. I was immediately sorry. What the hell was I thinking? Calamari, in the Georgia mountains, in a faux German Alpine village? I was obviously an idiot and that thought immediately dumped my mood even harder on a shitty day; that moment may be one of the few times in my life I can accurately describe as despair.

I'd gotten a Coke and it helped. I ordered a burger along with the calamari. Then the calamari arrived. It looked right, it tasted even better, and, actually, it was absolutely fantastic: Calamari steak sliced into fingers and lightly-breaded. Plus, the sauce was a sweet Thai chili sauce that was absolutely delicious. I inhaled it. The burger arrived and was cooked perfectly, and it came with great fries. I wolfed it down and, as I was leaving, decided to walk down the main drag in

Helen for a bit. I found a hand-dipped ice cream shop and got a giant vanilla milkshake. It was fabulous. Even the rain had stopped. I got back to the hotel room and collapsed on the bed under my draped hammock and passed out.

When I woke up in the morning it was pouring rain, and I smiled; I wasn't walking today, let it rain. A couple of hours later it stopped; I went uptown to Betty's Country Store to do my resupply. Not a great place for a standard resupply, but I got a sub, wrapped for the next day, and some other food that would work until my next resupply in Hiawassee. The store was really, really cool and had a lot of unique, locally-made foods. I bought some great snacks and found some cherry bite licorice that I love. The rain held off throughout the time I was doing my resupply and eating lunch. It rained again for a few hours in the afternoon, but stopped before I went out for dinner. It had been a really nice and restful day and I was ready to hit the trail again.

People will tell you a lot about the physical difficulties of doing a long-distance hike, but they don't talk nearly as much about the mental side of it. Zach Davis' book, *Appalachian Trials*, does a good job detailing what this is like and gives some tips on how to confront the mental challenge of the hike. It's important on the trail to keep your head right. I had times on the trail where I had to take a break, sit quietly and meditate, just to keep going for the day. There were times when I hung it up early, just to enjoy the day, because I needed the down-time. And at least one time I totally bailed off the trail for a couple of days because I just needed a break. Don't get me wrong, I loved my time on the trail; and, as I write this, I miss it more than you can understand. But you have to do what you have to do to keep yourself both physically and mentally healthy. In this case those damn calamari fries might have been the make-or-break moment for my whole trip.

CHAPTER THREE

March 15th – The Ides of March always hold a special sway for me; I had a great English teacher in high school who created a love of Shakespeare for me, and we read Julius Caesar multiple times. Additionally, it is the birthday of both my cousin, Jessica, and my maternal grandfather. It is a special day. It was also a good day on the trail; it started with the thing that was both the most beautiful thing I saw and the thing that made me happiest that day. That thing was the single most spectacular sunrise of my life. I woke up early in the hammock and lazily looked out toward the shelter and immediately my adrenaline shot through the roof. The shelter was on fire! Or so I thought at first; I unzipped and spun around and was about to grab my camp shoes when I realized it wasn't the shelter— but the sky—that was on fire.

The sky was flame-red, bleeding into an orange so bright that I wasn't surprised that I mistook it for an actual fire. I was totally blown away; I fumbled for my camera for a minute as the sky swirled from red to orange, with blue forming at the edges. I gave up on the camera, realizing it would never do the sky justice. I sat back in my hammock for fifteen minutes just watching the sky perform, while I listened to others wake up and react to the morning.

What I would learn during that day was to be more careful about assessing water sources. They'd been so plentiful so far and I'd been cutting things close. I briefly got burned because of it. Nothing serious, just about a half hour of walking dry, but enough of an issue to get my attention.

March 17th – It would take a few hours before I realized it was St. Patrick's Day. What finally tipped me off was the third hiker who passed me with a can of Guinness stuck in his pack. This was the day I was supposed to make the Georgia/North Carolina state line and the "fuck you" mountains. It was a long day up to the state line and the sign was a bit disappointing, it was small and on a tree at the edge of the trail. Still, it was my first state line and I was feeling pretty good standing there in the afternoon sun. The most beautiful thing I saw was a blue butterfly that landed on the sign while I was standing there. I hit the campground just past the sign and ate and took some rest while chatting with other hikers. I was trying to decide whether or not I wanted to do the next two climbs or stay there for the night. The story I've been told (and I don't know how true it is) is that the AT was originally supposed to terminate in NC not GA. So when the decision was made to make the terminus Springer Mountain, NC responded by making the connection point into NC two really hard climbs as a "fuck you" to the change.

While I was sitting there trying to make the decision, one of the several happy things of the day happened for me. A day hiker walked up and said, "Anybody want a Coke?" I pounced on it and thanked him profusely; the sugar and caffeine burst gave me what I needed to make the very tough climbs up to Muskrat Shelter. At the shelter that night I met both Appendicitis and Optimist, two hikers who would become fun hiking partners and great friends. I also met a really nice couple. The husband had attended Eastern Kentucky University where I went to graduate school. I would see them again some weeks later in the middle of the Shenandoah National Park (SNP). (It would be one afternoon, when a car pulled up as I was walking along the road and someone yelled, "Hey Rev, we've been looking for you." The couple had abandoned their hike but had been following me online. They were vacationing in the SNP and had been hoping to see me. They had snacks and a cold beer set aside in a cooler waiting just for me.) What I learned that day as I left Georgia was that I could hump for almost eight hours over some serious hills. Since I was heading into the big hills of NC and TN, this was good news.

March 20th – 21st – After a night at a hostel I checked into the Budget Inn for two days. The Budget Inn in Franklin is more preferable to the Budget Inn in Hiawassee. The owner, Ron Haven, is a wonderful and interesting fellow. My knees were bothering me a bit from having pushed too hard to get into Franklin, and my boots had gone to shit. So I ended up doing a double zero so that I could get my Merrell's shipped to me at Outdoor 76, a really great outfitter in town. I spent two days around that place and those folks were fantastic. They were knowledgeable, patient and friendly. I watched them spend two days dialing-in better shoes for Backtrack. Franklin was a fantastic experience, and we talked about it a lot amongst ourselves. Hiawassee was our first major trail town and it left a bad taste in my mouth. Everything we needed was there, but at a minimal level. For a town whose economy must be at least somewhat dependent on the AT trail community, it felt like people thought we were an imposition. People in Franklin, however, really seemed happy to see us and were very welcoming. Hell, I even got hit by a car in Hiawassee! A little old lady backed right into me as she was pulling out of the post office. Luckily, I saw the backup lights and slapped the trunk as she hit me. I was really lucky that she hit the brakes instead of flooring it, or this would be a much different book.

As happy as I was in Franklin, it was also the first time I started doubting my knees would make the whole trip. But I had a great time in town and I got to reconnect with some folks I'd previously meet on the trail; I met Lucky Strike and connected with Jedi, whom I'd met a few days earlier.

A Note from March 22: Do you love it?

So this question was put to me, "Do I love it?" and it was not an easy one to answer. Not because I wasn't enjoying hiking the Appalachian Trail, but because the experience was far too complex for a simple answer.

Each day on the trail often feels like multiple days. The perception of these splits can be driven by the weather, geography or the company.

Arriving in a hostel one night, a fellow hiker brought up a conversation we'd had a couple of days earlier. Except that we'd actually talked that morning at breakfast. But, he'd since had a camp morning, a short solo hike, and a rushed hike with a group to make a gap and get off the trail. Then he had hitchhiked into town alone before hooking up with us. Each of those activities could seem like a separate day. That, and the fact that you don't know what day it is, can often lead to completely losing track of what happened when.

So, for me, I'd been on the trail for two weeks but it seemed like at least a month. The majority of those days had been wonderful; many had been very hard, and a couple had sucked. Over that time, I'd done more unsupported backpacking than ever before, stretched and pushed myself in new ways, learned a lot, and met many fascinating people. So, my answer was complex: I was glad I was out there; I was excited by the challenge; and I was happy that the journey was continuing and I was having happy days.

March 23rd meeting Awesome – Wayah Bald to Waser Bald Shelter. I was hiking with Backtrack and we did a 13-mile day in the sun. The most beautiful thing I saw was a sight that would become fairly common in North Carolina: beautiful green valleys filled with clouds and/or fog, an advantage to being in the high hills. What I learned was that even through a 13-mile day in the high country, my knees did well when I took my time and didn't push. What made me happy was the overall good feel for the day; it was sunny and nice and we bumped into friends on the trail. But what I didn't know then, is that it would be a pretty important day. Backtrack and I hit camp near darkness and there were a couple of other folks already set up, including a couple of older guys. By older guys, of course, I mean folks my age.

We got to chatting, and one of them came over to say hi. He sat down and started chatting with us. His name, appropriately, was Awesome, and he smiled after one of us made a comment about some chasing. He then said, "Oh, you're cheese grater thighs?" We both looked at him, shocked. How could he have known about a conversation we had had earlier? He chuckled and said, in full southern drawl, "Y'all ain't the quietest hikers on the trial."

Backtrack and I burst out laughing. The other hiker soon came over and this is how we met Awesome and Kingfisher. Little did I know that this would end up being the unofficial first meeting of the AARP Gang and that these two would become what I believe will be life-long friends.

March 24th Wayah Bald Shelter to the Nantahala Outdoor Center (NOC). The NOC takes on the level of mythological lore on the trail for a couple of reasons. First, it really is a little hiker haven. There are places to stay, an outfitter, a restaurant, a camp store and a laundry—all within a few hundred feet of each other. The hike into the NOC is a beautiful run. You come down to a place called The Jump, which has a pretty gnarly descent. The most beautiful thing on the day was, not surprisingly, the view off of The Jump. However, it was a rocky day, and although I absolutely loved wearing my Merrells I noticed the differences between trail shoes and hiking boots. The trail shoes were much, *much* lighter and my feet did not heat up. What's more, hiking boots have hard soles whereas my trail shoes left me feeling many of the rocks on the trail—much more than I would like. My feet were getting sore from the impacts on the rocks. It's something I would eventually get used to and definitely not a reason to go back to heavy and hot boots. What made me happy was the descent off The Jump; I really stretched myself and expanded on what I thought I was capable, and felt really good to see my skill set expanding.

Lucky Strike and Jedi

So you meet all kinds of hikers with all kinds of interesting trail names. When I met Jedi, I had to ask how he got his name. Because at over six-feet tall, rugged, athletic and a former cop, he didn't strike me as much of a *Star Wars* fan. I also felt oddly comfortable with him almost immediately. It turned out he'd been given the name by fellow hikers who insisted that he had been playing Jedi mind tricks on them. Bam! There's your trail name. He'd actually been telling them, over and over again, that they were almost at camp—a little mind trick—to keep them pushing to camp.

I'd been hiking along at the same pace with Jedi for a couple of days when we started chatting around dinner one night. We quickly put together that we'd grown up about twenty miles apart in New York. At one point, he also tossed out his last name, and I laughed and said, "Funny, I went to law school with a guy form NY with the same last name." "What school?" "McGeorge." "Yeah, that was my twin brother," he answered. Suddenly, it made sense why I'd felt so comfortable around him. It turned out, in fact, that his brother was someone I hung out with in law school in California. It's a small damn world.

Oddly, I had just been telling Backtrack a story about Jedi's brother a couple of days before. You see, I often refer to myself as the second-whitest man in America. Jedi's brother and I debated who was whiter while on a rafting trip one day. So we decided to settle it having by both of us dive down to the bottom of the American River. Then, our friends on the raft would tell us who was more visible. When we got back to the raft, our friends told us that I was completely visible on the bottom and that they could see my arms, legs, and even my hands. However, they could count Jedi's brother's fingers! Hence, I'm the second-whitest man in America.

Not long after that, I was a day or two ahead of Jedi on the trail. As I was leaving Franklin, he was coming into town. I'd also met Lucky Strike the night before, and a few days later, as we were hiking into the NOC, he was sitting at the end of the trail with a sign that said, "Are you Jedi?" You see, the trail has its own network, and information moves up and down the trail at amazing speed. It's always been that way, but cell phones and social media have now made it lightning fast.

It turned out that Lucky Strike had lost his cell phone and had been told that Jedi had found it. I had to bum-out Lucky Strike by letting him know that Jedi was probably two days behind us. He was unhappy as hell, but what are you going to do? I wouldn't see Lucky Strike again until I got to Fontana. When I did, I asked him if he and Jedi ever crossed paths. He said no, but then he told me the most amazing story. It turns out that Jedi found the phone, and then used it to call one of the contacts. This happened to be someone who had just sent Lucky Strike a box. The box had gone to Franklin first, and was being forwarded to Lucky Strike up the trail. Somehow, Jedi had intercepted the box and got the cell phone into it before the box was forwarded. I love this story. The total coincidental nature of how it happened and the fact that I knew both of them but they didn't know each other, demonstrates the way hikers really do look out for each other and how they are part of one large trail family. And, of course, I love the happy ending.

March 25th We had spent a great night at the Nantahala Outdoor Center (NOC) and had formed the core of the AARP gang for the hike out. Backtrack, Kingfisher, Awesome and myself—all of us at or near fifty years of age or older—had a lot in common. We heard that the climb out of the NOC was a bitch, and that turned out to be the truest piece of trail gossip I'd ever heard. It's a brutal climb with few breaks, and near the top it arcs up a bit before finally letting you on top. It was another one of those climbs I like, however, for as steep as it was there was a pretty consistent slope. I ended up leading the way for most of the back part of the climb. The most beautiful thing I saw were lavender colored butterflies: beautiful, delicate little things I hadn't previously seen on the trail. The thing I learned that day was, old guys rock. It was a really wonderful day and a hell of a challenge for a bunch of old guys. It made me absolutely happy that we conquered that hill in the fashion that we did. The group broke up for the night on top, as Backtrack and I pushed on to a shelter further down the line. But the AARP group would stay together, grow, shrink, and become my core trail family on the trail.

I miss these guys and the rest of my trail family every day. We all shared some of the best times of our lives together and I will be forever grateful for their friendship, their company, their humor and good will.

A Note on Trail Community

The stories about Lucky Strike and Jedi, and the formation of the AARP gang, go to show how close the trail community becomes. We look out for each other, take care of each other, and help out when we can. I heard numerous stories of people forgetting things at shelters and, hours later, turning back for the shelter only to encounter another hiker coming up the trail to give them what they had left behind.

I get lots of questions about how safe it is for a woman to thru-hike alone. What I learned on the trail is that no one hikes alone unless they want to. Hell, sometimes it's hard to find time alone in the bubble. Not that we all hike in a big pack all the time. But you meet people all day, and anytime someone stops, you pass them by. When you take a break in the early days of the trail you have people walking past a lot. By Virginia, you've got dozens of hiking partners you've hiked with at one time or another.

The close-knit nature of the trail community surprised me; I never expected I'd end up being so close to so many folks that quickly. It really was a wonderful experience and something I miss dearly now that I'm back in the default world.

CHAPTER FOUR

March 27th - Cable Gap Shelter to Fontana. I was looking forward to getting to Fontana for a lot of reasons. I'd gone to school in TN and had been to the dam and lake and I liked the area. There would also be a nice hotel room and good food for a night, not to mention a box from home. It was a pretty hike down the mountain, catching glimpses of the lake. Those views, and the fields of wildflowers that were breaking out at the lower elevations, were the most beautiful things I saw that day. At one point, the sides of the trail looked snow-colored from a distance. When you got up close, you saw thousands of little white flowers. It was really spectacular and our first sign of spring. My knees were doing OK, and what I was learning was that I could do miles, could climb, and even descend well, without pain, as long as I didn't push myself too hard. What made me happiest that day was a working Coke machine at the base of the trail at Fontana Lake. Somewhere there exists a picture of me giving that machine a very happy and intimate hug.

March 30th – Birch Spring Gap to Spence Field Shelter. It was a rainy, cloudy day and the most beautiful thing I saw was the sun coming out. It would turn out to be a really pleasant day, but I was in a foul mood. We were climbing a lot and I was just out of sorts and knew I had to do something to get my head right. We took a break at a shelter and I excused myself and went off alone and just took five minutes to sit and do a simple breathing meditation. That was all it took; I felt better, my head was clearer and my focus was back. Hiking is so much more a mental game than you realize, until something like this happens. Knowing that, and knowing I could get myself right through meditating, was what I learned that day.

The happiest thing I saw that day was morning. The night before had been gnarly; we were camped in a campground covered with bear warnings, mediocre company, and widow-makers everywhere. I had found a good place to hang, but the weather turned sour. The thunderstorms that rolled through that night were the scariest I faced on the whole hike. There was lots of rain, really close lightning (the kind where the thunder rips almost simultaneously with the flash), and so much wind that I felt like I was sleeping in a boat instead of a hammock. In the middle of the night I heard a noise I couldn't identify. I stuck my head out to look around but couldn't see anything. I woke up in the morning, happy to be safe and alive. As I swung out of my hammock I saw what the noise had been. A thin, almost 40-foot tree had crashed into the middle of the campground. Amazingly, the tree had fallen in the opposite direction of a tent and two hammocks and had landed in-between the two sets of bear cables. Ironically, all the widow-makers I'd identified the day before were all still standing in place.

March 31st – Spence Field Shelter to Silars Bald Shelter. There are days on the trail when you look at the profile and you think, "OK, today won't be too bad," and you end up being completely and totally wrong. This day was one of the most brutal; it felt like we climbed forever. Plus, on the earlier pieces, the rate of climb kept varying, which is something I hate. As the day wore on, the climbing was gnarly but the rate got more consistent. So, yeah, consistently brutal. Kick-in the fact that water sources were spread out (and we completely missed one) and you have all the makings for a tough day. The AARP group was at its largest now, about ten of us, and when a day wears on you (like this one did), people's emotions get frayed. There were a number of times people erupted at each other. This was the only day I saw this happen on the trail, and it really underscores how hard it was as on us as we climbed toward 6000 feet. The only upside to the day was that it had been clear in the Smoky Mountain National Park, and when that happens you get some truly spectacular views. Those views were easily the most beautiful thing I saw that day. I really enjoyed the type of forest we got into in the higher altitudes, and liking the landscape helps your mood on a climb.

A secondary effect of an unexpectedly hard day is that you are also far slower than you had anticipated. So, what looked like a six- or seven-hour day on the trail was quickly heading toward a ten-hour day. Additionally, as the day wore on, the clouds started to roll in. With nerves in the group fraying, a couple of us who were doing well dropped the hammer and pulled ahead of the rest. Of course, in the mountains being just 10 or 15 minutes ahead can seem like forever. By the time we hit the shelter, the sky had gotten black and vicious looking. The shelter was packed and there were a number of tents set up. Just as we entered, the rain cut loose and it came down hard. Our friends behind us, already having a horrible day, were now being treated to an absolute soaking that would, as they got to the shelter, turn into a pelting as the storm turned from rain to hail stones.

It was a particularly hard day for one of our friends, who, to add insult-to-injury, would end up with leg cramps in the middle of the night. When I arrived at the shelter there were only a few spots left. I was done, and against my better judgement I claimed a spot in the shelter. I was dreading sleeping on my little Thermarest, or, more accurately, laying uncomfortably awake on it, and I was whining about it. It was at that moment that I learned that trail magic is ever present; I encountered the thing that made me happiest that day. A section hiker on spring-break started asking me about my Thermarest and then told me how much he hated his three-inch-thick air mattress. To my complete amazement he asked if I would like to trade for the night. I immediately said yes. I didn't get a lot of sleep that night, but the few hours I got would have been impossible without that big fat air mattress. It had crossed my mind that the kid was just being nice to an old man, but in the morning he was so happy he asked if I wanted to trade. I didn't do the trade; I figured I could pick up a lighter big air mattress for shelter nights. And, in fact, I did later. But that kid's kindness was an incredible piece of trail magic at the end of a really hard day, and another example of how nice hikers can be to each other on the trail.

Section Hiking

As opposed to doing a thru-hike, section hikers are folks who are doing the full Appalachian Trail, one section at a time. A section can be 40 miles or, in the case of LASHERS and BASHERS (Long-ASS, or Big-Ass Section Hikers), hundreds of miles long. These folks have my absolute admiration, taking years, and sometimes decades, to complete the entire trail shows a level of dedication I have a hard time imagining. In talking with them, they confirmed what I had already thought: about the time they got fully into hiking-shape, it was time to go home.

I really have a lot of respect for section hikers. Recently, I read a piece by a section hiker about why he loves and hates thru-hikers. It was an interesting piece in which he explained that he admires thru-hikers for being able to live out his dream, but dislikes them for looking down on him because he is a section hiker.

I think that perception is incorrect. Sure, there are likely some immature thru-hikers who hold that opinion. Some of the *hikier-than-thou* hikers look down on everyone not ripping 20-mile-plus days and for carrying less than 25 pounds in their packs.

However, the majority of thru-hikers I've spoken to share my respect for section hikers for a couple of reasons. First, the absolute commitment they display. Sure, thru-hiking means total life disruption for 6 or 7 months. But completing 2200 miles of trail, 60 or 100 miles a year, is a 20-plus-year commitment. Secondly, I respect their toughness. It takes some time on the trail to get your trail legs, but once you get to that point you are just dealing with wear and tear on your body. For section hikers, once they get to feeling good on the trail, it's time to go home. Then rinse and repeat, sometimes 20-plus times. That's incredible dedication. So my hat's off to the section hikers out there, and much respect.

April 1st Silar Bald Shelter to Clingman's Dome and Gatlinburg. This is the day we would hit the highest point on the Appalachian Trail at 6600 feet. We were excited for that milestone, as well as for the snack bar at the site, dreaming of Cokes and such. We had read that the observatory and parking area at the dome were opening that day. It was a really sunny and clear day, the clearest I've ever seen in the Smokies, and the views off of the peaks around Clingman's Dome were unbelievable—easily the most beautiful thing we saw that day. I was getting my climbing legs and my knees felt great. What I learned that day was that although I'm not the fastest hiker on flat ground, and pitifully slow descending, I could climb with almost anyone, particularly when there was a consistent slope. Coming off the trail into tourist hell was quite a gear-shift. The park was packed and we completely stood-out. People were very curious about who we were and what we were doing; we'd even get a little yogi-ing in during the walk. Unfortunately, the little store beat up our mood: no real food, no Cokes, just some water, souvenir chocolate bars, jam and honey. That list was NOT what we were hoping for in the park. Running low on food, we'd decided to try and hitchhike into Gatlinburg from the dome, and we were all able to get rides into town. What made me happiest that day, in addition to getting a great ride into town, was feeling just a little bit like a rock star with the tourists.

Yogi-ing

Yogi-ing is a particular skill that most hikers develop on the trail. It's the ability to be both utterly fascinating and utterly pathetic to the general public, at the same time. Your hope, and this really works best in State and National parks, is to spike people's fascination with what you're doing and engender enough sympathy that they pass on a little food, drink or a ride, in return for your stories. The concept comes from the old Yogi the Bear cartoons; Yogi was always in search of a lovely picnic basket purloined from the tourists in Jellystone National Park. My favorite day of Yogi-ing on the trail was in the Smoky Mountain National Park. We arrived at Clingman's Dome on the park's opening day. It was a beautiful day. We'd been on the trail for about four days and I was sooo looking forward to hitting the tourist store and getting a Coke. We emerged from the forest looking as shabby and disheveled as a thru-hiker can look. As we started to mix with the crowd, we were actually overcome by the smells of the perfume, shampoo and deodorant that wafted over us. One hiker actively started smelling people and saying just a bit too loudly, "Wow, these people smell great." Second Star and I quickly reined him in, pointing out that when you look like some hillbilly homeless guy who lives in the forest, you probably shouldn't be smelling people in public. It was a pretty funny moment.

On the walk down from the peak, we started conversations with folks. They were very curious about us. We were making connections—step 1 in a successful Yogi offensive. We hit the tourist store only to find they only sold bottled water and two types of candy bars, some jams and honey. It was utterly depressing. But we'd decided to go into Gatlinburg for a zero and we needed rides off the mountain, about 20 miles into town. That's where step 2 comes in—looking pathetic. So we lined up, about 8 of us, near the edge of the parking lot and started looking pathetic and putting out our thumbs. We had a few folks give us snacks but no rides. We caught a ride, one with cookies from one family we'd worked on the way down the hill. We would eventually all get rides, but the best part of the day was a mini-van that whipped over to us. Suddenly, fruit, candy, chips and cans of iced tea started coming out of the window, all at the hands of young boy who was about 10 years old. He was excited, and his mother asked if he could take his picture with us. Of course we said yes. We piled gear on him, a pack and poles, and then pulled him into the group. He was thrilled. I gave a card to the mom, and a few days later got an email from her in my Ministry of Happiness email account. The kid was beyond thrilled; his uncle had done a thru-hike and he already had AT-fever as a 10-year-old. He'd come to Clingman's Dome that day with the single purpose of becoming a trail angel. He'd been utterly disappointed, as all the way up to the observation tower and back he didn't see a single hiker. When he spotted us, he'd yelled to his mother to pull over! In her email, the mom told me he'd printed out his picture with us and put it on the wall. Sometimes, even when Yogi-ing, you give better than you get.

April 8th I had taken a trail vacation for a few days in Knoxville, where I'd gone to grad school. It was a nice break in a hotel, with a good bed, good food, TV and time to write. (A funny thing, during those two days in Knoxville, I found my first tick of the year on me—I didn't get it while out on the trail, but in Knoxville.) It had been time for me to get off the trail; hiking with a big group and being stacked-up with a lot of hikers in the Smokies left me no time alone. It had worn me down and now I needed a break. I would catch up with my group a couple of days later at Standing Bear

Hostel. We pooled funds while at Standing Bear and made a big spaghetti dinner—without a doubt, one of the best meals I had on the trail. The second day back out on the trail I realized it was definitely spring. Both coming into April and dropping elevation had done it. Suddenly, we were seeing lots of wildflowers and on this day I would see a whole hillside covered in flowers, easily the most beautiful thing I saw that day. What I learned was that after a few days off of the trail the first day back was fine, but the second day was rough. On this day, I had little energy or motivation and was very slow. The thing that made me happy that day was the thing that made Backtrack the least happy, his encounter with the North American Wood Snake.

Stump Bears, Tree Snakes and Things that Go Bump in the Night

So as you prepare to hike the Appalachian Trail and be out there for months at a time, people are constantly at you with their fears about the trail. Mostly these fears center around snakes, bears and outlaws. I was asked numerous times if I was going to carry a gun. No; I was (and did) not. I was asked how large of a knife I'd be carrying. "I'll be carrying, a pen knife," I would respond. These responses would get the most incredulous looks from folks. "Aren't you afraid?" they would ask. In fact, I really didn't fear the things they did. My biggest fears, as I've related, were widow-makers, lightning, ticks and mosquitos. Of course, that doesn't mean I'm not fearful of bears and snakes. Black Bears are not to be horribly feared and are rarely seen outside the Smokies and the Shenandoah National Park. But there is that first moment when you spot one and you go all tingly inside. Most of my bear interactions (I only had three) were very brief. Twice, a bear popped up on the trail, looked and me, and then continued on its way. The most nerve-wracking encounter happened in the Shenandoah and I never even saw the bear. I passed a SOBO who told me he had seen a momma and cubs up the trail. That's always a little hairy. I kept an eye out as I was moving, and at one point could actually hear the cubs. Unfortunately, I was now on a part of the trail with densely-packed, chest-high brush on either side. A few seconds later, I heard momma bear. She barked twice at me—

from closer than I would ever want to hear a momma bear bark. I kept talking to her, "Moving right along momma, no need to be nervous, be gone in a minute, momma." It was a tense couple of minutes and probably more dangerous than I realized. Luckily for me, she had likely been between me and the cubs and was just letting me know I should keep moving. I took her advice.

Snakes I expected to be a far bigger issue. Rattlesnakes are not uncommon on the trail, and many folks in camp related stories of sightings, and some even talked about stubborn rattlesnakes which refused to yield the trail. The fact is, over the three-and-a-half months I was on the trail, I never saw one. Like my bear encounter, I did hear one as I stepped next to a pine tree in Massachusetts. My body reacted before my mind, propelling me straight up in the air and quickly forward. I like rattlesnakes. I like any creature that gives you sufficient warning and a chance to walk away. The nearest I came to snake injury was on a mountaintop in Virginia near Damascus. Flying along some very flat trail, my body once again reacted before my mind had time to process. I'd half-passed a snake when it moved. I again found myself flying up in the air and quickly forward. A quick couple of steps later I turned to see that it was a six-foot-long rat snake. I did not know they got nearly that big. It was mellow, and I got a good picture of it, but it damn near gave me a heart attack. Search the web and you may be able to find the picture of the rat snake I later saw on Twitter; that one must have been ten-feet long. Seeing one like that might have actually killed me.

So, while you're on the trail you have bears and snakes in the back of your mind. That's true particularly at night in your tent or hammock, and especially when you're camping alone. When you're camping alone everything sounds like a damn bear. One night, just as I was about to fall asleep, I heard a noise that sounded like a stick breaking. It jolted me awake but I let it go. I was alone at the shelter site when I had crashed for the night and it was not uncommon for a hiker to come in later and set up. When the second stick cracked closer to my hammock I called out and got no answer. I called out again. My nerves now started to fray a bit and I grabbed my only weapon, my LED headlamp. I waited. When the third stick cracked it sounded like it was a foot from the hammock. I blasted out of the hammock wearing nothing but my boxers, light blazing. I jumped up on the big boulder next to the hammock, waving the light around furiously and yelling at . . . nothing. Not a damn thing anywhere. No sounds of running, no critters, nothing. Just me in my boxers, barefoot on a boulder. Eventually I climbed back into the hammock and tried to relax. I took a Tylenol PM and finally (it was now about 3AM) started to drift back to sleep. Just at that moment, when I was dropping off to sleep (you know, the point when you often get the falling sensation and wake back up), something smacked the tarp on my hammock and my body literally raised up into the air before coming crashing back down in the hammock. During my brief flight, my brain had caught up and processed the situation. It had been one of nature's most deadly torments—a falling acorn. I felt like a total idiot, and as the adrenaline coursed through my body I began to laugh at myself. I was also more awake than at any moment I had ever been on the trail. Sleep was lost, so I got up. I rarely ate much for breakfast on the trail, but at about 4AM that morning I made a full meal and ate a leisurely breakfast and then lit back out on the trail at dawn.

As terrifying as the deadly acorn attack had been, I did not have to face the trail's most terrifying creature; that hell was reserved for my friend Backtrack. First, a little background about stump bears: You see, trees sometimes grow oddly and create burls. These lumpy outcroppings look amazingly like small bears clinging to the trees. These, along with stumps, cut logs, and various rock formations, conspire to convince you there are bears everywhere. The worst thing is, you usually catch them out of the corner of your eye, which gives you a quick adrenaline burst on the trail (followed almost immediately by a couple of minutes of berating yourself for being an idiot).

One afternoon, while walking up a particularly long climb in the Smokies with Backtrack, I heard the most hideous scream I have ever heard from a human being on the trail. I turned quickly, fully expecting to see a mountain lion riding my friend's back. But there was nothing. Backtrack had, in that second, plopped himself down on a log and just sat there shaking his head. I looked up, and saw above him a vine swinging back and forth. I immediately knew what happened; he'd been attacked by the North America Wooden Tree Snake (NAWTS). The attack is rarely fatal, save the occasional heart attack. This is to be expected, as vines do not have teeth. To my friend's dismay, I burst out laughing hysterically and was unable to stop laughing at him until well into the next day.

I have been attacked myself. What happens is, you're moving along, head down, watching the ground so you don't trip on a root or a rock, and the NAWTS pounces on you from above. Ordinarily it's a brief and unsuccessful attack, quickly hooking and releasing your pack. It startles you, but it's usually no big deal. Backtrack, however, suffered the most insidious type of attack; the vine hooked his pack and instead of releasing, slid around the side of his pack and head, as if it was crawling. As silly as it sounds, it really does feel like something crawling around your head. This is what accounted for a six-foot-three-inch, two-hundred-and-seventy-pound man screaming like a ten-year-old-girl in a haunted house. Beware the NAWTS friends, they're coming for you.

April 9th Into Hot Springs. This was probably the most wonderful time on the trail; we had an easy downhill run into Hot Springs that day. It was a trail town that would finally live up to the idea I had in my head as to what a trail town was supposed to be. By that I mean that it was small, walkable, and welcoming. It had a decent outfitter, plenty of spots for resupply and good restaurants (the wings at the Spring Creek Tavern were some of the best I've ever had). It is also the home of the hiker ministry, a place to hang out, to refuel (physically and spiritually), and a place of immense kindness (and very often, freshly baked cookies). The wildflowers continued to reign as the most beautiful things I saw each day. On this day, the group was keeping a pretty torrid pace, but at one point I pulled back and slowed down. The forest above Hot Springs was open with a lush green carpet of foliage, dotted with amazing wildflowers. So I slowed down, took some pictures, and just really enjoyed the moment of being there. What I learned that day was how to better handle the dynamics in my group. I was finally getting to know folks and how to deal with each of them. I would pick up my pace again and cover the last three-plus miles in an hour. The trail was gently sloping, relatively free of obstructions, and at points I was nearly running down the trail. It was fun to be feeling good and to be on a perfect trail for moving fast, particularly with the expectation of a Coke at the end of the run. The thing that made me happiest that day was walking up on Laughing Heart Hostel and seeing familiar, friendly faces, as well as a cold beer (not quite a Coke but it worked for me in that moment).

Four Trolls on a Bridge

So, on the trail this day, at a point where the trail crossed a little stream over a footbridge, a tall, pretty, young blonde woman came down the hill. There, she found four older, sweaty hikers taking a break on the little bridge, just sitting there, hanging their feet in the water. She smiled and said, in the sweetest little southern drawl you've ever heard, "Lookie here, four trolls on a bridge."

It was said in good humor and we all laughed. She stopped and chatted for a few minutes. She lived nearby and was out for a day hike. She was absolutely beautiful and, of course, after a month on the trail almost anything she said was charming, and she was excessively so.

As she walked by, I found myself slightly enchanted and turned to follow her. I began to think about the river scene from *Brother, Where Art Though?*. I wondered if she was a land siren and if I followed her up the trail would she perhaps turn me into a toad? Such is life on a hot sunny day in North Carolina on the Appalachian Trail.

April 13th We started the day moving pretty well, all of us, except for Backtrack. His knees had been getting increasingly worse along the trail. The group was pretty spread out and we had seen in the guide that there was a "mom's store" just off the trail. Coming down a hill, there was suddenly a hand-written sign: "mom's store 100 yards." This was the most beautiful thing I saw that day, as I was really in the mood for something other than the food I'd been carrying. The store was great. It wasn't much, a store-front with a couple of coolers, freezers, a microwave, and a crockpot for hot dogs and chili.

We hit the store about 9:30 in the morning and tore into a round of breakfast treats, including my favorite, little chocolate donuts. We quickly turned to sodas, and then we microwaved hot pockets while gently enticing one of the owners to get the hot dogs started. Hot dogs, of course, followed. We soon ran into a hiker several of us knew, who told us that Hemlock Hollow Hostel just up the trail was a pretty decent place to stay. The rain clouds that had been forming (and were now occasionally spitting) made that idea sound pretty good. But we'd only been walking a couple of hours, so we decided to move forward. We slid down the road and waited at the crossing for the rest of the group to come along. Eventually, after a much longer time than expected, we saw Backtrack hobbling down the trail. Jedi looked at me and said, "We need to get him to a doctor." I agreed; it was pretty obvious he was in a lot of pain and discomfort. So, what I learned that day was plans on the AT can change at the drop of a hat. We decided to hit Hemlock Hollow and create a plan to get the big guy to the doctor. We'd spend a day-and-a-half at Hemlock Hollow before getting Backtrack up to Johnson City and the doctors. Our stay at Hemlock Hollow was beyond interesting and I will tell you that Hattie, who owns the place, makes some damn fine biscuits and gravy—the first really good biscuits and gravy I'd had on the trail. (I've heard that recently Hattie sold the place.) What made me happy that day was getting to Hemlock Hollow and knowing we'd be getting Backtrack some help.

April 14th and 15th Uncle Johnny's Hostel, Erwin, TN. We got a ride up to Erwin from a trail angel who fortuitously had come into Hemlock Hollow for lunch on the first day, and awho greed to drive us up the next day. Erwin is close to Johnson City, where we knew Backtrack could see a doctor and an orthopedist, if need be. Our time at Uncle Johnny's was awesome. We rented a couple of cabins, and all of us piled in and, after making a Walmart Run, we made community meals and watched some movies on the DVD player. All three of my questions were answered by the same thing that day: our group. It was a beautiful little trail family; we learned how to take care of each other and make everyone happy. Like any family, we had our moments of strife, but it was a great group. If I seem nostalgic writing this it's because Hemlock Hollow was the last time that group was together. A couple of folks had hiked past Hemlock Hollow toward Erwin, while the rest yellow-blazed up to get Backtrack to the doctor. Backtrack would later get the news from the doctors that he'd need several weeks before he could get back on the trail. But it wasn't enough and he would never be able to hike with us again. So we had been nearly ten, but the next day, when we walked out of Erwin, there were only four of us remaining in the group.

CHAPTER FIVE

April 17th Second Star and I camped at the base of Mount Unaka, which initiated a bit of silliness in me. We were at the base of the mountain and the Japanese-sounding name inspired a theatrical outburst in classic mythological Shogun style. I screamed, "Mt. Unaka! We come for you at dawn!" And we did; the morning was cool and foggy and, once again, Second Star showed that she was a much faster hiker than I, as she soon disappeared up the mountain. I was taking my normal, slow and steady pace through the fog. The hill was surprisingly tough and it was a long, slow climb for me, but enjoyable. The payoff was one of my favorite moments on the trail and which resulted in my best photo for the trip. The top of Mt. Unaka was a magical spot that morning: light and fog in the pines, the sun breaking through in individual rays; it easily could have been a mountain in ancient Japan. At any moment I expected samurai to explode out of the forest and into battle. But it was peaceful, incredibly so, and I sat down and soaked it in for a time. All of my questions were answered right there; it was perhaps the most beautiful spot on the whole trip. I was reminded that hard work has its payoffs and I was incredibly happy sitting there in that quiet magical place. For me, that moment is why I hike; why I pushed out on the AT, and why I spend time in nature. No television show, no movie—no book, even—can impact your very soul like a perfect moment in nature.

April 19th The beginning of the end. I had spent the night at Over Mountain Shelter. It's a huge converted barn with two levels, two sleeping decks, and space for at least forty hikers. It was magnificent, and one of the few times I was actually OK about sleeping in a shelter. The lower decks had views down the valleys and the prospect of waking up to that view was exciting. I shared the shelter with a troop of boy scouts and one other hiker; they all opted to sleep indoors in the upper level. That left the bottom decks to me, alone, and it was one of the few nights I got any sleep in a shelter. I woke just before first light to a rain shower that was suddenly getting blown into the deck. I slid my gear back and sat there watching the sun try to break through the clouds in the valley. As it became light, I could see the storm coming up the valley and decided to make a break for it over the Humps—the two mountains next up on the trail. I had a reservation at Mountain Harbour B&B, and for a couple of hundred miles I had listened to Awesome talk about breakfast at this place. So I was anxious to finally get there. What I didn't know is that the Humps were not just nearly five-thousand-foot-high hills, they were also balds. So, instead of walking through trees in the storm, I was completely exposed. Heading over those hills had been a bad decision all the way around.

The storm I thought I'd stay ahead of was moving much faster than I'd anticipated, and it caught me early on the first climb. The fog was heavy. Most likely, I was walking in the lower clouds of the storm. The temperature was tanking down into the high thirties, the wind was picking up, and the rain was dumping. Initially, this was just another day on the AT in the rain. My gear was working well. My jacket and rain skirt were keeping me dry, even if the wind was blowing hard enough to pin them both to my body. I realized I had made another mistake by not eating enough in the morning, and now stopping to eat wasn't going to be an option, at least for a while. There was very little, if any, cover on the mountain and the prospects of stopping to eat on the trail in the middle of bald, over five thousand feet, in the pouring rain, was not appealing. So I pushed on and the track went from damp, to slick, to muddy, to a damn river. So I started walking the clumped grass at the edge of the track.

What I would soon learn about the Humps was that they are full of false summits. Every ten minutes, when I thought I was hitting the ridge, I'd cross it only to see another one coming. My mood was heading into the well—because, I'm sure, of the weather, my mistakes and my dropping blood sugar. I was finally on the second hump when the wind did a one-eighty on a dime and blew open my rain skirt, allowing the rain to soak me to the core. I had no time to get it spun around and refastened. Soaked, I kept moving, and the temperature continued to drop. The rain that had been hitting the side of my head started making a new sound, a result of it starting to freeze. As it turned to sleet, it was being blown so hard that it started to feel like someone was shooting me in the head with a BB gun. I was now cold, wet, and hungry, and stopping was completely out of the question. I was starting to seriously get concerned about hypothermia.

That's when it happened.

Hiking is an utterly mindful pursuit; lose focus and you fall. And that's what I did. I was stepping on a grass tuft and the wind caught my foot and pushed it just far enough to the left that I slid off, twisted my foot, and spiraled to the ground wrenching my left knee in the process. It hurt—a lot—and I knew this wasn't one of those things that I would just walk off. I wanted very much to lay there and rest, let the pain and throbbing subside a bit; but dying of hypothermia is not the best way to cure a knee injury. I got up and started hobbling forward in pain. It was at about this time that it hit me that I was about as far away from being the Minister of Happiness as I could be. So I stopped for a few seconds and decided to get my shit together. Yes, I had at least five hundred feet of climbing left to do; yes, I was soaked, hungry and in pain. I was basically miserable. But that was not a reason to be unhappy. I could walk, slowly, but I could move. I'd get over the hill; I'd get some food. I had a bed at a great B&B waiting for me and I was hiking the Appalachian Trail on what easily could be considered the adventure of a lifetime. What reason did I really have not to be happy? So I decided to sing. Why? I have no idea; but somehow, in that moment, it seemed like the perfectly rational thing to do to raise my mood. I have no memory of what I was singing as I walked, but I know I was screaming it out with Viking-like enthusiasm as I hobbled up that hill in the fog and the rain.

Of course, no spoiler here, I did make it—but with one last insult. On some hills, the AT has an annoying habit of having to touch the absolute highest point, even if the trail just walks out and back to the point. It did this on top of the second hump. I walked a good hundred feet out and back to a point ten feet from where I had turned. The singing did, for a small period of time, turn into a string of obscenities directed that ATC, the trail clubs, myself, and anyone else I could think of who was responsible for me being on the trail. The swearing stopped when I hit the tree line and finally got out of the rain and the wind. I stopped a few hundred feet down the trail. I found a rock overhang, out of the pouring rain, and ate. My knee hurt like hell. I didn't stop long; I was really afraid if I did my knee would tighten up and I wouldn't be able to walk. The odd thing, however, was that in that moment I was so proud of myself. I'd conquered that damn mountain under seriously shitty conditions, even though I was hurt and hobbling. For the first time on the trail I felt like a badass thru-hiker. Ironically, at the exact moment, that signaled the death of any real chance that I'd complete the full thru-hike. The most beautiful thing I saw that day was the Mountain Harbour B&B. I'd learned about the one weakness the rain skirt possessed. But I was happy at having really overcome a terrible day. When I got to the B&B and knocked on the door, the look on the woman's face was priceless. She just stood there for a minute, speechless, before she said, "Let me get you a laundry basket for your things." I must have been one hell of a sight.

Awesome had been right, the breakfast buffet the next morning may have been the best breakfast of my life. While at breakfast, a hiker I knew asked me about my noticeable limp so I told him the story of my injury. Another hiker at the table said, "Thank you, I thought I was going insane." Apparently, I hadn't been as alone as I felt on the mountain; he'd been a short distance ahead of me in the fog and had heard my insane singing (which, to him, in the wind, had just sounded like some crazed harpy swirling around and singing in the sky).

I did a short, four-mile slack pack back to the hostel the next day, and rested as much as I could before I left one of the nicest B&B's I've ever been in. I also felt very lucky; another hiker staying at the hostel had fallen in nearly the same place, and in much the same way, the day before. His hike was done and he would later end-up having to have surgery on his knee. So, although I was hurt, and the injury would eventually be enough to derail my thru-hike, at least I wasn't done at that moment and I wasn't heading under the knife. Perspective is a wonderful thing.

April 21st Two days of rest at Mountain Harbour B&B had done my knee a world of good. It felt a little weak, but the pain and stiffness had receded to almost nothing. I had planned a fifteen-mile day over terrain that didn't look too bad, with only a bigger climb near the end of the day. I wasn't concerned about climbs; I was concerned about downhills, where my knee would struggle. It was late in the afternoon when I hit the shelter where I had planned to camp and I didn't like it. It was a little shelter with little vegetation and lots of graffiti inside. Honestly, more than anything it just had a bad vibe.

I sat down and realized I was only six miles, almost all a fairly gentle downhill, to Bob People's place, the Kincora Hostel. My friend Jedi had told me about Bob and I'd seen the famous graffiti in the shelter, "Jesus asks Bob's People's what to do." So, even though I knew I'd be pushing daylight and a 21-mile day, I decided to go for it. Two younger hikers had arrived and were also going to be heading out, but I got off about five minutes before they did and started pushing. There was one big uphill and then a downhill run for the rest of the hike. I quickly realized a couple of my assumptions were wrong. First, I'd assumed that, given the terrain, it would be a quick run. It was not. The trail was very rocky, and because I was still a little unsure of my knee I had to be really careful. I was, however, making pretty good time. But I was descending into a valley and even though the sun hadn't set it was soon disappearing behind the hills. Now adding to the complexity of the run was seriously diminished daylight. When I finally hit the road to make the turn to Kincora I had expected that the hostel was close to the road. It was not. So it was a much longer walk up to the hostel than I expected. It had been a very long day, but I opened the door to find Jedi sitting in a chair reading a book. It was good to see a familiar face. I would find three more at the hostel, including one who gave me her dinner leftovers as I'd arrived at almost 8PM. Bob has cats. I'm allergic to cats, so not the greatest night for me; but the Kincora mailbox was certainly the most beautiful thing I saw that day. (Sorry, Jedi.)

I learned that my knee was better than I had feared, but it would only be a temporary reprieve. I woke up the next morning with a heat rash where my socks had covered my leg—a result of the long day. What made me happy that day was putting in a big day. Twenty-one miles would be my second-longest single day (although I likely did more than 22 by time I got to the hostel). I was also happy about staying ahead of the two younger hikers on the descent. It made me feel good to beat a couple of young bucks down the hill. Now, if you are reading this and thinking, "Hey, that was me and my friend!" please do not contact me and let me know you guys stopped for tea three times on the way down the hill; let an old man have his illusions and his moment.

April 22nd Into Damascus. This day would be an easy hike but my knee was really sore. The long day before might have gone well but it was a really stupid move on my part. Backtrack was rehabbing his knee in Damascus (actually up in Abingdon) and I decided on the way into town that I'd probably take a couple of days there to do the same. I was looking forward to Damascus, the home of trail days. I expected it to be a really great place to hang out. I was actually a bit disappointed; it was a nice enough place, but I think I'd built it up far too much in my mind. The outfitter in town, Mt. Rogers Outfitter, was absolutely awesome, with really knowledgeable, nice, fun folks. The most beautiful thing I saw that day coming into town was the view down the valley toward Damascus. What I learned was that the trail had the effect of calming me down; I was more relaxed, and I was not as jumpy as I normally was. This showed up in a couple of ways: normally, when tapped on the shoulder in the dead of the night, I come up swinging. Not this time. I was also not getting startled by critters as much, even snakes. What made me happy that day was meeting Underdog. One thing that happens on the trail is you hear a hiker's trail name again and again, but never meet them. I was eating lunch at a shelter when she came in. It was great to meet her and she was super-nice. We discovered that day that we both hike at the same speed, which, given our height (and therefore difference in leg-length), means she's a much better hiker than I am. I heard she completed her thru-hike successfully and that makes me really happy.

Answering Second Grader's Questions

Before I left for my hike, I visited two elementary school classrooms and talked to them about hiking the Appalachian Trail. The students were great and asked really good questions. They got a kick out of my rain skirt and how I would do laundry. And, of course, the idea of pooping in the forest was hugely entertaining for them.

I kept in touch with them via postcards, and while in Damascus, VA, I received a pack of letters from them. The letters were wonderful and they once again asked a ton of questions. Here are some of their questions and my answers:

Where are you?
I'm currently in Damascus, VA, 468 miles from where I started.

What animals have you seen?
Lots of birds, several snakes, a deer, a fox, a turkey, mice and a mole.

Are you having a great adventure?
Yes I am; it has been amazing.

Is anyone being mean or laughing at you?
Everyone has been really nice and friendly.

Have you made any friends?
Yes, I have made several really good friends.

Do you know people in the towns you go to?
Most of the time, I don't; but people are usually very nice to hikers.

How much money have you spent, are you running out of money?
I have spent about $2000, and I still have enough money for the trip.

Can you still walk or are you pooped?
I'm not pooped and am still walking, even though I have hurt my knee. I get tired but I rest up when I go into town.

What is the best thing you have done?
I really loved climbing and being on top of Mount Unaka.

Do you look funny doing laundry in your rain skirt?
Yes I do.

Have you taken a shower?
Yes, I have been getting at least one shower a week.

Is your hammock comfortable?
Yes it has been warm, dry and comfy.

What do you do for entertainment?
I talk with other hikers and sometimes I listen to music in my hammock.

Have you been in any storms?
Yes, I have been in a couple of scary thunderstorms and in a rain storm with 40-mile-an-hour winds.

Have you seen any boats?
The trail hasn't been close to any big lakes or rivers so far, so I haven't seen any boats yet.

Did a bear or any other animals steal your food?
No, so far I'm the only one eating my food.

Is your bag still heavy?
Yes, about 35 pounds, but it was 42 when I started so it is much lighter now.

Are you homesick?
I miss my friends and family but I am having a good time and am not homesick.

What are the mountains like?
They are beautiful and big; some are really rocky and most are peaceful and quiet.

How long is your beard?
Long enough to blow around in the wind and even hit me in the eye!

Damascus April 22 – 27th In Damascus I planned on taking a double zero and buying a knee brace, then I waited an extra day to hike out with Mad Hatter, who'd come into town. *Then*, I took five days to rest up and get my knee ready. It was a great time reconnecting with Backtrack, who was holed-up there, rehabbing his knees. It was great seeing Mad Hatter, Second Star, and some other folks who came through. I even got to have dinner with Kara and Jimmy—two really close friends (and two of the nicest human beings alive). On the 27th, I proved once again how stupid I was: I decided to have Backtrack slack pack me and Mad Hatter, and I did a 21-mile slack back into town. Why I did 21 miles I have no idea, and it completely changed my philosophy about slack packing.

As a thru-hiker you have a tendency to slack longer days than usual because, of course, they are easier days with no weight on your back. Plus, you want to make miles. Of course, that ends up meaning those days aren't really rests; they are just good mileage days. Since then, for the most part, I started doing normal length slack packs so that I could get miles, but also get a bit of a rest. My knees did OK for the day, but the long day caused another heat rash, so I would have to change from my SmartWool socks to socks with no wool content. I have a wool allergy, but my SmartWools and Darn Tough socks had never bothered me before. What I deduced was that on really long and warm days hiking anything over eighteen miles caused my legs to sweat, and the wool fibers were able to penetrate my liners and irritate my legs. Along with the heat, this gave me gnarly looking rashes. I switched to Wigwam's made out of Coolmax, and on hot days would sometimes go with only my liners, which worked out for me.

I decided to hike out the next day, but the weather report didn't look good. Mad Hatter went out ahead of me but I ended up hanging in town for another of couple of days. Partially to rest my knees a bit more, partially out of laziness, partially to hang with Backtrack who I realized would likely not get back on the trail. And, finally, I stayed because I wanted to avoid some bad weather.

May 1st – Backtrack took me back up to White Mountain from where I had slacked back a few days earlier. As we were heading up the mountain, the ground looked weird and we soon realized that it had snowed on the mountain. So, I started out that morning on top of a snow-capped mountain on a grey day. It was a tough morning, having to say goodbye to Backtrack for maybe the last time. Then, hiking on a snow-covered trail with snow plastered to the trees, it was hard to see white blazes. The snow on the rocks made the trail slippery as hell and, thankfully, I was the second person through that morning and had a set of tracks to follow. But it was May, and as I started to descend a bit the snow was soon gone. Not much later I hit the boundary for the Grayson Highlands, home of the famous pony herds. I saw a lot of hoof prints and scat piles, but no ponies. I stopped for lunch at one of the shelters and was getting really annoyed with the highlands. The trails are not very good and the two things everyone raves about—the ponies and the amazing views—were not present on this grey and cloudy day. But there were plenty of rocks. I would get a glimpse of why people love the highlands; the most beautiful thing that day was the sun breaking out of clouds and lighting up the valleys. Unfortunately, it was a fleeting pleasure.

What I learned that day was that my rest in Damascus had been a good idea; my knees felt good. Just as I was nearing the northern boundary of the highlands I crossed over a rock ridge in the fog. On the other side, I was startled by a pony I'd climbed down next to. I would soon make out in the fog that I'd walked right into the middle of a herd. As I went to take out my camera, one of the ponies nuzzled me thinking I was bringing out food. As much as I made fun of others getting so excited about the ponies, it made me really happy to see the highland ponies.

May 2nd – 3rd Two really pretty days on the way to Marion, VA. I did a 19-mile day with little knee pain and no heat rash, so the new socks were working. The days were filled with beautiful views. I saw waterfalls and I took a lovely break to sit along the Holston River. I didn't sleep well the first night and wasn't eating well. I could feel it as my energy level dropped off. You would think I would have known by this point how important sleep and food are to having the right energy and mood while hiking. But I learned that all over again. What made me really happy over those two days were successful miles with little pain, my socks working, and hitchhiking into town.

A funny thing happened while hitchhiking; two white-haired old ladies slowed down like they were going to pick me up, but once they got a close look at me they punched the gas and took off. I was both pissed off and amused; I guess I pretty much looked like a homeless serial killer at that point, so I really couldn't blame them. I got another ride soon enough, found a place to stay, and bought a bus ticket. I had plans to meet Second Star in Washington, DC—a place I'd never played tourist before, and someplace I was really looking forward to seeing.

May 12th More than a week off the trail in DC, and other places, meant that strapping on a pack again sucked. But we were starting at the southern end of the Shenandoah National Park and we had relatively easy terrain. Plus, there were camp stores and waysides to look forward to as we went through the park. The first day was lovely and there were beautiful things everywhere: flowers all over the trail, yellow metallic-looking little spiders and green metallic-looking beetles that were both beautiful and truly alien looking. What I learned that day was that about three days should be the maximum length of a trail vacation; any more than that and you really feel like you are starting over. What made me happy was getting back on the trail and the sweet smell of spring forest soil.

May 13th My hike had really changed; my knees were sore the whole week I was in DC. I walked down stairs like an 80 year-old man the whole time. I'd started to dream that I was recovering well enough to consider making the full length of the trail. This day I would really start backtracking on that idea as my knees hurt all day (and it was an easy day). The wildflowers were in full and massive bloom and were the most beautiful thing I saw. The realization that my knees likely wouldn't let me finish was the big realization for the day. What made me happy was seeing my first bear on the trail. One second I was clipping along and the next second—bam!—there he was, popping onto the trail in front of me. He was not large (I guess 200 pounds) and was about a hundred feet up the trail. He didn't sense me and I wish I had thought to go for my camera first, but I clicked my poles and he was up and out. The Shenandoah National Park (SNP) reportedly has the highest concentration of black bears anywhere in the world. Given that every night in the park multiple people had bear encounter stories, you can believe it. Want to see black bears? The SNP is your place.

May 16th The most beautiful thing I saw this day was a field full of pink flowers; it was up-slope from the trail in an open patch. This whole day would be a massive sensory experience; the forest was in full bloom and the smells were incredible: flowers, trees and that damp loam smell the ground has in the spring. Our pace had slowed down ridiculously from thru-hiking standards. It really had become about the smiles and not the miles. My knees were OK but I realized pushing no longer made sense. The main impact of this realization was that I knew I wouldn't finish the thru-hike; I knew I should slow down. At that point the goal became maximum enjoyment because I now truly had internalized that my time on the trail was a limited and precious commodity. My hope was to skip over Northern PA and get into the Northeast where I grew up. It was a happy day with good breakfast; we'd been in town for the night and we got a free ride back to the trail. The hike for the day saw us make it to the most fully-stocked and wonderful camp store I'd seen on the trail, and just minutes before the rain started dumping.

How to Negotiate with the Wild Thru-hiker

After I'd hurt my knee the first time I knew my chances of completing a full thru-hike were limited. I had started out with bad knees and, indeed, I had injured my left knee further. So, this meant I was much more focused on the journey and not the destination. Basically, it was time to be more concerned with smiles than the miles, a natural fit for someone who writes a blog called The Ministry of Happiness. In the Shenandoah, on a particularly hot day, we'd hit one of the waysides early, and, after two breakfasts and a milkshake, I really didn't feel like moving. My hiking partners were in a similar mood, but Second Star found some motivation and lit-out for camp.

We only had about six miles left for the day. Sitting at a picnic table with a section hiker we'd just met, I started joking around, wondering how pissed Second Star would be if we yellow-blazed up the road and beat her to camp. It was at that moment that the section hiker said, "What if I told you I already have us a ride?" It turned out he'd just met a woman who was driving a little RV and who was supporting her husband, who was thru-hiking. She'd offered him a ride, and after a quick check-in she was game to take all three of us a few miles up the road to a short, one mile-hike from camp. I immediately knew we were going to do this, I also immediately knew Second Star was going to kill me in my sleep that night. My only hope was that I had spotted her favorite variety of Sam Adams in the wayside store. So I went in and bought her a bottle. Then, in an attempt to increase my odds of not being murdered in my sleep, I wrapped the beer in my Mylar sheet to try to keep it cold.

We arrived at camp and were there for a time. We had decided to start a fire but the area near the shelter was pretty much picked clean of firewood. So we were making ever longer trips out into the trees to find more wood. At one point, while picking up some wood, I could feel eyes piercing through my head. I looked up; it was Second Star glaring at me from 150 feet away. I gingerly approached her. Some advice here, when approaching the angry thru-hiker in their natural environment: it's highly advisable to approach in a calm, quiet manner, speaking in a comforting tone and, as soon as possible, offering gifts. This was the approach I took; she immediately said, "You're dead." I had pre-set the environment by making a note in the shelter journal about my amazing and wonderful friend, Second Star. I pointed her to the entry as I made a rear-guard move to my pack before she could strike. She looked up from the journal and I added quickly, "What if I had a beer for you?" She glared. "A cold beer," I began unrolling the Mylar. "That would help," she said. "A cold Sam Adams," I said, showing her the label. "My favorite," she replied. "I know," I said tentatively. She took the bottle, looked at me and said, "You can live." And this, my friends, is how you negotiate with a thru-hiker in the wild.

May 19th – The new attitude made everything better in the SNP. There were beautiful views of the valley all day along the trail. What I learned that day was that in the middle of May, with massive hours of daylight, flat trails and no real need for pace, you can still do a sixteen-mile day without hurrying. It was still a long day, but it included breaks and snacks and stops to just sit and enjoy the sun.

The thing that made me happiest that day was coming into a park and seeing two section-hikers we'd met the night before—two absolutely sweet, absolutely beautiful girls from Virginia. We hung for a few minutes at a picnic table before they moved on. I was content, however, to lie on that picnic table and just stare at the clouds. It was something I used to do a lot when I was a kid, and I wondered how many decades it had been since I'd last done that. It made me sad that it had been so long. It was the realization that the pace of life gets away from you; you no longer find the time or the value in just stopping and realizing the beauty and the miraculous all around you. I would stay on the bench through visits with three other hiker friends before I'd finally got up and finished the last miles of the day's hike. But I count that time on that picnic bench as some of the very best time I spent on the trail.

May 21st – Destination Front Royal, VA. This day would be the last day in the SNP and it was pouring rain. It was mostly a downhill run and I had, at various times, several different hiking companions. The most beautiful thing I would see would be the red pickup truck that would give me a ride into town. What I learned that day was a reminder that under the right conditions, I really like walking in the rain.

This was one of those days; it was raining fairly hard, but it wasn't cold, my gear was working and the trail was in pretty good shape. Under those conditions walking in the rain is downright pleasant. Sound is muffled, and the colors of some flowers pop out even more in the rain. It was a really wonderful walk. What really made me happy that day was that a fellow hiker, Mau, who knew my knee had been hurting, purposefully slowed down to stick with me after he had caught up to me. I finally had to force him to move on ahead at his normal speed, but it meant a lot that a guy I'd met a couple of days before would automatically extend that kind of kindness. This is what hikers do for each other, but Mau was kinder than most.

Mau was hiking to honor another marine, a friend who had died stateside after coming home. I'd get to know Mau a little bit, and his walk in support of the "Jason Kerella Hike for Higher Ground Organization" was truly inspiring. The group's website is at http://karellahikeat.org, and is a worthy group that honors our fallen veterans and helps disabled veterans and their families. There were a lot of veterans on the trail and I had a lot of respect for them before my hike. But after getting to know some of them a lot better, I have a bigger spot in my heart for them.

CHAPTER SIX

May 24th – 25th The highlight of these two days would be meeting my
favorite little hiker, a nine month old little girl. She did 300 miles on
the AT in 2015 and she hadn't even started walking yet. So what's
your excuse for not doing any miles this year? We would camp with
her and her parents at one shelter and then at the beautiful Bear Den
Hostel. These two days would also be the infamous Rollercoaster, a
fourteen-mile section of ups and downs that you hear about while
you're on the trail because of the giant pain-in-the-ass it is for hikers.
Oddly, I would do the first ten miles the first day and would be fine
the next morning. But I learned that even ten miles can be a really
long day. We would do the last four, plus some additional miles, the
next day, and then set up before heading down into Harpers Ferry.
The things that made me really happy were the comforts at the Bear's
Den (it was really wonderful) and getting to hang out with my
favorite little hiker; she's a fabulous little kid.

My Favorite Little Hiker

One of my best memories on my hike was hanging out with a nine
month old hiker. I first met her walking into camp in Virginia and I
immediately cringed; the idea of having a baby in camp who might be
crying all night did not make me happy. Mom, dad and baby were
sitting in the shelter so I decided to set up camp as far away from the
shelter as possible. What I hadn't counted on was that they were
considerate parents and had also decided to set up camp as far away
from the shelter. So—you got it—we were neighbors for the night.

I love kids and after setting-up as almost everyone did, I went over to
meet the little monster who I'd envisioned would be keeping me
awake all night. She was an absolutely adorable and incredibly happy
baby. I would end up camping with the family for two nights, and
then be with them another night in a hostel. Over those three days I
never heard her cry.

I talked about this with her mom one night and her explanation for the lack of crying (and why she was so damn happy all of the time) really seemed spot-on. First, she was getting hordes of attention; every hiker wanted to say hi and entertain her and make her laugh. When they were hiking, she was set up high in her pack seat and had a great view of the trees, other hikers and vistas. Plus, being high up for long periods of time is pretty rare for a baby. There was also a lack of negative stimulation, particularly in terms of noise—no city smells, no loud car doors or alarms, and none of the constant urban noise we usually have to put up with.

This became something I really noticed this summer: how unbelievably loud towns are—not just large cities, but every town we entered, no matter how small. We live in an environment where things are NEVER quiet. Even indoors we have refrigerators and heating systems, traffic going by, etc. Have you ever noticed that when you turn on your TV early in the morning the volume is really high? That's the effect of having noise all day. By the end of the day, our hearing has readjusted and we turn the TV up. This little girl was facing none of this, and at night had a really quiet, calm environment to sleep in with her parents.

I spoke with her mom recently and she told me that my little friend is starting to walk. So, yes, my friends, she did 300 miles on the Appalachian Trail before she could walk! You have to love that about her and I see many happy days in her future.

May 26th I would wake up this morning, a beautiful morning in the hills above Harper's Ferry, swing around, step on the ground and immediately fall back into the hammock. My knee felt like nothing was attached, like all of the bones were just floating inside of the skin. I could stand, I could walk forward, but any side-to-side movement meant immediate and sharp pain. It was a really depressing moment; the Rollercoaster had done me in and any fantasies I had about actually finishing the thru-hike were finally dead. I sat in my hammock for some time just sort of numb about it all, until my bladder forced me up and out of the hammock. I explained the situation to my hiking partners and started out early. I figured it would be slow going and since Second Star normally blew by me within the first hour I thought I'd get a head start. The crazy thing is that everything sort of fell into place; the trail was a gently slope downhill, it was clear, and where it wasn't there were flat, not-sharp rock fields to get across. I didn't need to do any real lateral movement so I was actually making good time. I mean really good time: I was humping nearly three miles-an-hour down the trail, a result of good trail, adrenaline and a lot of ibuprofen. The prettiest thing I saw that day was the way the forest opened up when I got near Harper's Ferry. It was beautiful. What I had learned, of course, was that my hike in the bigger sense was over. What made me happy was the sight of the Appalachian Trail Conservancy (ATC) office and the promise of air conditioning and cold drinks. I would be thru-hiker number 276 to hit the ATC in 2015. (Although I felt a little bit like a fraud signing-in as a thru-hiker, as I was pretty certain I would not be finishing.)

That day was a hard, emotionally. I felt like a failure, like my body had let me down. I had some time at the ATC office waiting for my hiking partners. I had a good conversation with a couple of thru-hikers from Australia, went through the books, ate some snacks, had a Coke. But even though my knee hurt, it was my mood that was suffering the most. I had gone through 10 miles on the first day of the Rollercoaster and had been fine. It seemed so unfair that the last 4 miles had done me in; it made no damn sense. My friends arrived and we had a great night in Harpers Ferry. But the next day I boarded a train to head for New York to rehab my knee.

June 13th – Back on the trail after rehab. My rehab included about 10 days staying off my feet. I went to Cape Cod for a few days and just sat on the beach. I visited with family in New York and then eased into walking a couple of miles each day. I did one test hike with a pack on: flat ground at Lake Taghkanic State Park in New York. I was excited about getting back onto the trail for a couple of reasons. First, I terribly missed trail life, and my knee felt pretty good, which allowed me to start fantasizing about finishing again. Second, I'd be doing a test hike for a week and would be hiking with one of my best friends, Bryan. We'd gone to college together at SUNY Plattsburgh and this would be the first time in a very long time that we'd get to spend this kind of time together. We decided to do a section from Bennington, VT down to Lee, MA. We set off on the trail, immediately facing a three-hundred-foot set of wet rock stairs. I, the big AT hiker, after having done almost seven hundred miles that summer, was feeling a little bit superior. I fell on the first climb. Yup, I fell going uphill on the rock stairs and severely bruised my ego. Thankfully, that was the only real injury from the spill. The most beautiful thing I saw that day was my first white blaze on the trail; it was good to be back. My learning over the week would be very knee-focused and for the first day my knee felt good. We hadn't done a long day, about seven miles, but we'd done some good climbs early on and I was doing well. What made me happy that day was finishing the day in good shape, setting up camp and getting into the hammock before the waves of mosquitoes drank me dry.

June 14th – Vermont is a really beautiful place and the AT through VT is no exception. The Long Trail passes many little lakes, and the first one I passed that day was absolutely spectacular. I was wearing a fairly heavy brace on my knee and although it was working fine there was a little chaffing going on, so my learning for that day was around how to reduce that. The highlight of the day, the thing that made me happiest, happened early in the morning. Bryan and I had camped on the other side of the stream away from the main area around Congdon Shelter. In the morning, Bryan was over by the shelter when I heard him say, "OK, I'll send him over." When he got back to camp he said, "Did you ride to Amicalola with someone named Survivor Dave?" I nodded and he said, "Somebody wants to say hello." I crossed the stream and saw three very thin versions of the guys I'd ridden into Amicalola with back in Georgia. I had started by staying in the lodge and then the Hike Inn, so they effectively had a two-day head start on me when we started. That head-start would be enough that I never caught up to them, until that morning. It was great getting reacquainted, and it was a wonderful surprise. Unfortunately, by the time I thought to get a photo with them, one had already hiked out. But I got a photo with the remaining two, a wonderfully happy trail reunion.

June 16th – We'd penetrated MA and would climb Mt. Greylock that day. Unfortunately, it was a rainy and foggy day. We got rained on several times and I have to say, even in bad weather, the Peace Tower on Mt. Greylock was an absolutely beautiful sight. What I would learn that day was how my friend and I differed in regard to rain. Bryan was paying close attention to the incoming storms on his phone; I was, as usual, basically ignorant of what was coming. At the edge of the summit of Greylock there is a "day lodge," basically a shelter you can hang out in during the day but can't overnight in. It is particular useful, I imagine, in the winter for cross country skiers, but it served our purposes that day. We decided to wait out the storms there and it was a very happy decision. We snacked and chatted and I passed out for a couple of hours. It was a nice break from the weather and would allow us to finish the day without getting soaked, a great call on Bryan's part.

June 17th – As beautiful as it was, let me bitch for a minute about the Long Trail and the trails in Northern MA. They suck, at least at the time of year I went through. They were rocky as hell, wet and slippery (Bryan and I both would fall multiple times). There were downed trees everywhere and generally hard trails to hike. Alternately, the landscape was just beautiful. So, it was terrible footing with beautiful country as the tradeoff. The most beautiful thing I saw that day was a field littered with small purple flowers that were being fed on by hordes of little brown butterflies. The scene was something out of a Disney nature movie—nature at its best. During the day, while walking through a field, I would roll my ankle and go down. It was a little traumatic for a second; I fell in much the same way I had on the Humps when I hurt my knee so badly. I sat on the ground, stunned for a moment, not wanting to test my knee and having all kinds of negative thoughts blowing through my head. I got up and I was fine. Maybe I was learning how to fall better; maybe I was just lucky that day. Either way, what I learned—what was reinforced for me that day—was how important it was to really enjoy every minute on the trail, because it could all end in a heartbeat, a nice parallel with life in general. What made me really happy that day was taking lunch along an absolutely beautiful beaver pond.

June 18th - We decided to compress our week by a day and that meant pushing through a sixteen-mile day. Luckily, we did it on the nicest weather day of the trip. The sun came out and it was one of those puffy, white, cloudy days that alternated between grey and sunshine. The most beautiful thing I saw that day was Warner Hill. The trail opened up into these fields that were just covered with grass. The fields would lead up and around to a hilltop that was totally covered in the biggest damn blueberry bushes I'd ever seen. We were there a couple of weeks early for the berries to be ripe, but each bush was loaded with thousands of berries. I imagined the hill would be black bear central in a few weeks. The hill also gave a great view out to the mountains; the Peace Tower on Mt. Greylock was just barely visible. What I learned that day was that my knee, with brace, was still capable of handling a long sixteen-mile day. What made me happy was getting a little frustrated and doing something stupid in the last hour, which was pushing my pace. I'd done a good job all week of taking things easy, but I pumped out a near three-mile-an-hour pace over the last two-plus miles. It made me happy I could still do that without pain, and even happier in the morning when I was still pain-free. We would make Highway 20 our jumping off spot the next day; it had been a great week but it was time for food and showers and a real bed. What I learned that day was that I could continue; my hike wasn't absolutely finished.

Of course, the week had gone so well I would start allowing fantasies of finishing the whole trail to start to creep back into my psyche. What made me happy that day was just reflecting on a great week. I'm a gypsy; I've lived all over the US, and. as a result, my good friends are strung all over the world. It is rare for me to get a full week of one-on-one time with a really good friend; it was wonderful and one of the best parts of my entire AT experience.

July 2nd – I'd taken a couple of weeks off after the week on the Long Trail to give my knee a rest. This was my first day slack packing south in MA. My plan was to slack all of MA and part of CT before getting back onto the trail full-time. It was getting very hot and the idea of doing a few hours every morning seemed like a great way to get miles done, avoid the heat, and help my knee slowly strengthen. I was using my mother's place as a base, and she was kindly dropping me off to hike back to my car each day. She also caught the trail angel bug after giving rides to a couple of hikers. The most beautiful thing I saw this day was a stream, colored copper by tannins running out of a beaver pond. What I learned I was learning again: starting up after two weeks off the trail is very hard. I also was feeling more than rusty, but actually out of hiking-shape. This was a great hiking day. It was good trail and I got to do something I'd always wanted to do. You see, growing up, the first way I ever found out about the Appalachian Trail was by riding in a car on the Massachusetts Turnpike. There is a bridge-crossing that has a sign that says Appalachian Trail. As I got older and started hiking it always sat in the back of my mind that I was going to walk across that bridge someday. Someday was July 2, 2015.

July 3rd – A really cool day hiking with my eleven year-old nephew. The most beautiful thing I saw this day was my nephew standing in front of his first white blaze. He did really well on the hike; he started out flying and I think he was nervous because I let him lead. But once he found some bear sign on a tree, he slowed down. What I learned that day was that my map and guide reading skills were as rusty as my hiking skills. I miscounted the length of the hike and what I thought would be a short, four-mile hike turned into an even shorter, two-and-half-mile hike. But it was a happy day, hiking with my nephew, eating wild grapes and hopefully inspiring another generation of AT hikers to get out and hike.

July 9th One of the nice things about slack packing south was that I was running into hikers I had started out with when heading north. It was nice to get a taste, each day, of the community I was no longer involved with like I was before. It's one of the reasons that I think going NOBO in the spring is the best way to do a thru-hike. Flip-flopping, or going SOBO, you just don't get the same level of community as you do when you go north in one of the big bubbles. However, that was the highlight of the day; the stretch I was on— Route 7 to Route 23 in Massachusetts—was absolutely bug hell! For the first time in my life I actually broke out my head-net and put it on. The most beautiful thing I saw in hell was lots of really pretty fungi. During my time on the trail I'd become a big fan of all the amazing mushrooms and other fungi you see on the trail, and there were a lot of different ones that day. Being that it was the first time with a head-net on, I had a bit to learn and it was initially very uncomfortable. Eventually, though, I got used to having it on, to the point of basically forgetting it was there. It was around this point that I learned it's a really bad idea to spit while wearing a head net, because you feel like an idiot afterwards. It had been a brutally hot, humid and buggy day and what made me happiest was hitting the lot and getting in my car minutes before a thunderstorm opened up.

July 12th – I was finally on the trail full-time, heading south through the last bit of MA, and it was a nervous and exciting day. I was worried about my knee and my overall hiking fitness, but also was excited to be back out on the trail and to be back sleeping in my hammock. The views off of Jug End, shortly after I started, were absolutely amazing and they were the most beautiful thing I saw that day. What I learned that day was my heavier knee-brace was not going to be an option. First, on hard climbs it would start to dig into the back of my knees and I actually ended up with sores and cuts. Second, if I tried to counter that weight by using the light cotton braces underneath, the heat caused heat rashes.

So I settled for wearing just the cotton braces and carrying a heavier brace in case I got into trouble. What made me happy that day was running into a hiker I had never met before but about whom I knew a lot. My friend Kara had been telling me about another friend of hers who was hiking with her dog. As I was climbing up the edge of a small rock face I came face-to-face with a little dog. When the woman called it back I immediately knew who they were. It was a lovely little meeting in the forest and really made my day.

Brassie Brook Shelter

Sometimes on the trail you just hit a place that really works for you. One of these places, for me, was Brassie Brook Shelter in Connecticut. I had been back on the trail for about three days and that particular day had been a good one. I hit the shelter fairly early around 1:30 in the afternoon and decided to eat lunch and then figure out if I still wanted to continue. The odd thing is that two shelters, Brassie Brook and Riga, are only a tenth-of-a-mile apart. Riga is a bigger shelter but Brassie Brook had more camping space, so I opted for the latter. Good choice! The shelter area was in a Hemlock forest, a recent straight-line wind had cut a path through the camping area so there was one area of big downed and broken trees.

Just over the hill that led down to the shelter there a small cave. It was off behind the shelter in the rocks. The shelter was tiny with a little picnic table out front and there was a nice little view that included a stream off to the side.

I sat down at the table and ate lunch and took in the beauty and the peaceful nature of the spot. The stream had little waterfall sections that made it easy to fill bottles and allowed me to do a little clean-up. The quiet was broken by the bark of a big dog across the stream; I figured it must be at Riga Shelter. A few minutes later the dog came over the hill to the shelter, a powerful pit bull pulling his owner down the hill. I'm not the best with aggressive dogs. I put a hand on a trekking pole and prepared to dread the next few minutes. Then I saw his tail wagging like crazy.

The dog turned out to be a former military service dog and he was both drooly and incredibly friendly. He also chewed everything in sight; he destroyed a brand new tennis ball in about 3 minutes; he bit through a quarter-inch stick, and gnawed off a branch nub that was a good inch in diameter. His owner was equally interesting, a recent veteran who was dealing with some issues. I dropped into counseling mode and we had a really great talk for an hour or so. It was a good meeting in a wonderful spot.

I decided to spend the rest of the day at the shelter and hang my hammock in the Hemlock forest. It was a really amazing spot, and I had a lovely day lounging in the hammock and a wonderful night's sleep. Just one of many really special days on the trail.

July 13th – It was turning into a bloody hot summer! I got out of camp early to avoid the heat and was treated to two beautiful things, great views off of Race Mountain and tons of little toads all over the trail. But, as the day wore on, all of my thru-hiking dreams burned up in the sun. It was incredibly hot, I was chaffing everywhere, and heat rash was developing. I hated this small section of the trail. The area around Mt. Everett was filled with nasty little rock face climbs, the worst I'd faced on the trail. Honestly, I was thrilled I wasn't descending them. They sucked! I realized between the heat, my lowered fitness level, my knee, and my diminishing attitude, that it was truly over. This thought had occurred to me other times on the trail but this time I knew there would be no chance for the fantasy of finishing to creep back into my head. It wasn't just a physical consideration, I'd finally lost any mental drive I had to try and complete the thru-hike. The upside to that was that all of the pressure was off; I could do a two-mile day if I wanted, or lay around in camp all day. It was small consolation in the moment as the realization made me quite sad. What made me happy that day was running into more familiar NOBOs, finishing MA, and taking a break at the amazing Sage's Ravine.

Prettiest Place on the Trail

This statement is likely to start a bit of a lively debate as there are many amazing places along the Appalachian Trail. A lot of things impact how we perceive the beauty of a spot on the trail. The time of day, the season, and the weather have a lot to say about how a particular place looks. A disclaimer as well, I hiked a little less than half of the trail (1000 miles) so I've got a lot more to see to make any kind of definite statement here for the whole trail.

Along the trail from Georgia to Vermont there are many big views, these included Blood Mountain in GA, Clingman's Dome in the Smokies, Rocky Top, Mary's Rock, Jug End, and too many others to name. This list of course misses all of the little unnamed spots we hit at the right time, on the right day, in the right weather, that just stun you in the moment. It also excludes places like the Humps, which some people love but which I crossed in a forty-mile-an-hour storm that included hail and me hurting my knee. Conditions can be everything.

I will say that one of those "perfect moment" spots for me was Mt. Unaka. It was a special morning; we'd screamed challenges at the hill the night before at the end of a long day. The climb was steep and hard, but the payoff was a summit reminiscent of Middle Earth or ancient Japan. Making the summit and finding this magical place, I just sat down and let it embrace me.

There had been amazing sunsets and sunrises while on the trail and the best one I didn't even try to photograph. I woke up in my hammock one morning and thought the shelter nearby was on fire. When my sleep-filled eyes adjusted, I realized that it was the sky, not the shelter on fire. The sky was burning, pink and orange, more brightly than anything I've ever seen. It was a spectacular show of color that I almost couldn't believe was real.

You get a lot of trail talk about amazing places you're about to come upon. One of the most talked about is Max Patch, a huge bald with three-hundred-and-sixty-degree views. Personally, I didn't find Max Patch all that exciting, and even less so once we missed the first blaze on the base of it and got lost for twenty minutes.

However, once I got near the MA/CT border, I started hearing about Sages Ravine. Hikers were talking about it because the weather was brutally hot and humid and you could get in the water there. I was also told it was beautiful. In this case the spot matched up to its billing. The Ravine is a magical spot; it is deep in shade even on a hot summer day, and there is a small river, with short little waterfalls running into cold pools where you can sit in the water and cool off— an absolutely fabulous spot. I failed to photograph my favorite spot in the ravine as I went through. A little fall splits around a natural rock bench so that you can sit with water spraying on either side of you, while you dangle your feet in the river. Sages Ravine will be forever burned into my brain as one of my favorite AT location memories.

July 14th – It was another in a string of hot days and I was happy to be moving early. The most beautiful thing I saw was a gorgeous little brown butterfly with yellow wing tips; the cool thing was, we were moving along at the same speed and the butterfly hung with me for almost five minutes. I had made a mistake in the morning and had not dealt with the chafing that had started the day before. I would learn how much of a mistake that was because near the end of the day I was in a lot of pain. So I decided to pull off to a shelter that showed to be a couple of tenths of miles off the trail. What the guide didn't mention was that it was at the bottom of a mountain. I walked far too long only to hit a point where I still couldn't see the shelter, but where I could see blue blazes down another ravine and going up the other side. I decided to just hang my hammock on a flat spot off of the trail, but got annoyed because I didn't have water at that spot. Totally frustrated, I took a shot and called a hotel in Falls Village, CT. They had a room, way too expensive, but the idea of air conditioning, a restaurant, a shower, and a bed sounded too good. I was also supposed to be hooking up with Backtrack in a day or two; he was going to slack me in CT for a few days. So, even though I was not excited about hiking another five miles with a flaming crotch, I headed for Falls Village.

On the way down to town I ran into another Twitter friend and that bumped up my mood. I also knew that the bridge into Falls Village was out, so I figured I had a long hitch into town. What I didn't realize was that the whole "bridge out" thing was a giant cluster. I stopped a couple of local folks on the road and some didn't even know how to get to Falls Village. Luckily, a fellow hiker's husband was picking her up and they gave me a ride into town. Normally, this is no big deal, but let me tell you something about Falls Village, CT: it has the worst cell service I've ever encountered. The hotel lets you use their landline to make calls because service is nearly non-existent. This issue would show up while trying to get into town, as we couldn't get enough bars to get our navigation software to work. At one point we caught a signal, pulled over and hand-drew a map; this was a good move as we lost signal immediately after that. If the hotel hadn't had Wi-Fi, I could have easily been convinced that I was in a Twilight Zone episode and had woken up in 1950's CT. There is almost nothing in that town. There are only a couple of restaurants, and they have limited hours; there is no resupply, and, personally, I would skip right on by it if you're on the trail. A note on the Falls Village Bridge: the bridge repairs have concluded and so the trail once again allows you to walk more easily into town. But, honestly, I still wouldn't stop there.

July 16th – This was my first day slackpacking with Backtrack. After he could no longer hike on the trail he went back home, bought an RV and came back to play support crew for a bunch of us. As I wrote earlier, he's one of the kindest humans I've ever met. It was going to be an easy day; seven miles back to Falls Village. But, of course, we were kind of guessing on the road crossing. We guessed wrong and my seven-mile little hike turned out to be thirteen miles. So much for my new, take-it-easy slack-packing days. On the trail I met some new people and one of them pointed out some America Chestnut saplings. I knew that the chestnut blight had decimated them decades ago but wasn't aware that saplings still rise up to a decent height before they get the blight. It was both the thing I learned and the most beautiful and sad thing I saw that day. What made me happy was that for the first day in quite some time the humidity levels had dropped, so it was a really pleasant day walking on the trail.

July 18th – Optimist and Appendicitis had joined us the night before and we were slacking in opposite directions, with plans to meet up just outside of Kent, CT. It was an absolutely brutal day, probably the hottest and most humid day I'd encountered on the trail. At the halfway point I seriously considered bailing out. But there was no phone service so I decided to suck it up and keep moving. When I finally got to the road, it turned out I hadn't been the only one with that idea. I was, however, the only one who had kept going. The most beautiful thing I saw that day was a massive rock formation; it looked like a tiny version of half-dome in Yosemite. Unfortunately, the climb up next to it was pretty gnarly. What I learned that day was that I had staying power, having done the full hike in the heat and humidity was another one of those moments on the trail when you push yourself and find out what you can accomplish. What made me happy that day was running into a fellow hiker I hadn't seen in a really long time and also finding and eating my first ripe blueberries on the trail.

Appendicitis (Tough Cookie) and Some Jersey Boys

The next bit has been graciously contributed to me from my buddy Appendicitis. She told me this story when we were in NH and I was laughing so hard I told her I had to have it for the book.

Trail Journal Entry 6/25 at 3:54am: OK, so right now I'm sitting in my tent giggling because of something that just happened. Like I've said a couple of times now, the hike through NJ has been a personal favorite so far. However, New Jersey hikers have not fallen into my good graces for the following reasons: they set up their tents crazy close to ours and get roaring drunk, which explains why I'm writing this post at 4 am. Anyways, the funny part about being a seasoned thru-hiker is that very few noises scare me out here anymore. Not so for the New Jersey boys. Earlier, a barred owl was hooting off in the distance and they were getting all angsty because, and I quote, "those coyotes sounded really close".

Now, I can't blame them too much for that because when I first heard a barred owl I thought it sounded something more akin to a cackling witch/monkey hybrid. But the next thing was what really set me into fits of stifled laughter. It was getting cold in our tent, and we had sent home our sleeping bags due to the warmth at night and the need to shed weight off our packs. So if I get cold, I have to get out an emergency blanket, which is basically like really thin tin foil, and wrap it around me. But . . . it's really loud to unwrap. So, the second I pull it out and start unwrapping it, the Jersey kids immediately starting lighting up the area trying to figure out what animal is making that noise. I can hear them calling out, "Hello?" and "What the hell do you think that was?" And from now on, any move I make under the blanket, they are on high alert. I guess I could've announced myself, but I think they deserve to get a little spooked for keeping me up all night. Totally worth the flashlights being shined in my direction all night.

CHAPTER SEVEN

August 21st – I'd pulled the plug on being on the trail for a month, the main reason simply being it was too damn hot to hike. In the meantime, I'd gone north to do some day hikes in New Hampshire and Maine. I spent a good chunk of a day up on Mount Washington catching up with some fellow NOBO's I knew. I'd also readjusted my goals: what I was focusing on was doing at least a thousand total miles on the trail and also hiking in each state on the trail, even if it was just a day hike. Over the month I'd hit the states I hadn't hiked, and all that was left was to finish up my thousand miles. I planned on going back to Harper's Ferry and hike north back to Kent, CT, where I'd finished up slack packing. That would leave me well over my thousand-mile goal. That seemed like a good plan.

The first morning leaving Harper's Ferry was a bit surreal; first, a major fire had hit the city since I'd been there a few months before. Places where I'd expected to buy supplies were burned to black skeletons. The morning I headed out, I got lost looking for the foot bridge across the river, a minor inconvenience on a truly spectacular morning. The temperatures weren't bad and the sun was shining. The most beautiful thing I saw that day would repeat itself many times: the rays of the sun being broken into sprinkles of light across the surface of the river.

The first few hours that day were along the river on the utterly flat canal path: river on one side of the path, pools of water on the other. Almost every log in the pools had turtles sunning themselves; every puddle on the trail had frogs. I was learning that after a month off I could still hike; I knew I was not in hiking shape but I had been working hard in the gym so I wasn't useless when I got back out on the trail. All-in-all, the whole day was what made me happy. I realized I had gotten a taste for life on the trail when I had been off for a month. I had no idea how much I would miss being out there, how much I would crave the companionship of my trail family.

This is a sentiment I see in former thru-hikers all the time on social media. Life on the trail is simple and wonderful, the default world offers us complexity and anxiety in huge doses and it makes us crave that simpler time. This was the beginning of the absolute end of my hike and I was determined to appreciate every damn minute of it.

August 22nd – I knew that the second day back on the trail was always a tough one for me, so I was smart about the day; I slept-in a bit, took a lot of breaks, did an easy eight miles and pulled into a hiker's campground in the early afternoon. It was nice on day two; in the campground I was able to relax, read, and take a shower. Sitting in camp I had a swallow tail butterfly land on my trekking poles, a simple and beautiful moment. I met a lot of folks coming through that day and was reminded again of how fascinated folks are with the idea of thru-hiking and thru-hikers in general. What made me happy that day was just being smart about things, taking it easy and really enjoying a beautiful day on the trail.

August 23rd – The heat came roaring back and I'd planned a fairly easy ten-mile day. I passed on staying at Annapolis Rocks after taking a nice long lunch there and chatting with the caretaker. I felt like I should do at least ten miles for the day and the campsite I was planning to stay at was pretty much a downhill run. Of course, upon arriving at the Pogo Memorial Campsite I realized that had been a big mistake. This was, by far, the crappiest campground I'd encountered on the trail and I felt bad for whoever it was named after. The site is right on the trail; it's small with very little flat ground or good trees for hammocks. Initially, I was bummed because there was a bad water source. Happily, a couple of day hikers coming up an adjoining trail pointed me to an awesome water source on a side trail.

It was decision time; I considered heading back to Annapolis Rocks but the double-slap of backtracking and doing it uphill killed that idea. I decided to push on another five miles to the next shelter, but the guide said there would be little-to-no water there this time of year, and AWOL was dead on point with this prediction. Smartly, I'd loaded up with water at the campground, but now I was doing an unplanned extra five miles with an extra two liters of water on what was turning out to be a really hot day.

Such is life on the AT; you have to be flexible and ready to improvise because you just can't plan things to the numbers. One of the things we did a couple of times in camp was to have my friend, Second Star, pull out her AT Guide. She'd planned out the entire trip, day-by-day, in the guide; we'd pull it out and laugh at where she was supposed to be that particular day and how many miles she'd planned for that day. It was funny because there are so many assumptions you make about the trail before you head out—assumptions that quickly fall apart. For me, I'd always been horrified by how few miles people averaged per-day during a thru-hike, and then, of course, I fell right into those same averages.

The most beautiful thing I saw that day was a church at the first road-crossing of the day. It was one of those picturesque spots: an older, simple wooden church on the hill, looking out over rolling fields. The church and the fields shining in the morning sun were truly spectacular in the simplest way. What I learned that day was that even after a month off I could still reach down and grab another five miles at the end of the day. I'd learned this early on, I truly believe that no matter how hard the day has been, you can reach down and grab another five miles at the end of the day if you need to. Now, those miles might truly suck and you might be miserable, but we all have those kinds of reserves in us. And that was what truly made me happy that day, accomplishing those last five miles with the extra water on my back.

August 24th – This was the type of day you dream of on the trail. I woke up early and it was cooler than I expected. The trail was good and it was one of those days when you have just hit it right; you ate right, you slept well, your body is responding well, and you feel like you could hike a hundred miles. I was taking my time and strolling at a leisurely pace. I met a few section hikers on the trail who were really interesting and friendly. The most beautiful thing I saw was a gorgeous stream that came out of a meadow into the forest. I happened upon it at the perfect time for a lunch break; it had perfect rocks to sit on and spread out. I spent a good long time hanging out there. What I learned wasn't much of a revelation, but slow-paced easy days are heavenly. Later in the day, I was getting ready to climb up to a road crossing and I saw a creature in the stream. I was reminded of Gollum from the Lord of the Rings. At first glance it looked like a drowned zombie-rat crawling over the rocks, but your eyes play tricks on you. It had ducked behind a couple of rocks when it saw me. I had to know what it was, so I sat down and waited. Eventually, it stuck out its nose, and finally crawled from between the rocks. It was the biggest damn bullfrog I've ever seen in my life. It was huge. It had some vegetation stuck to one shoulder and had a bit of weird color for a frog. But, for some reason, sitting there watching it made me so damn happy. Later in camp I would encounter a group from Gettysburg College and would spend some time talking with a couple of the students. The chats turned into mentoring sessions with a couple of great students and that gave me a taste of the one thing I missed about my job, working with bright, young students.

August 25th – I would finish Maryland this day, arriving at Pen Mar Park fairly early in the day. I'd booked a room at the Burgundy Lane B&B in Waynesboro, and I made the call to get picked up by them at the park. It's always a bit nerve-wracking going into these situations; it's hard to know how hiker-friendly people are, especially if it's not a hostel set-up. While waiting, I sat in Pen Mar Park, and the most beautiful thing I saw that day was the view out of the park looking down over Pennsylvania. The owner of the B&B arrived and I immediately got a good vibe from him. I've mentioned this before, but I was not on a typical "just scraping by" hiker-budget, and since my birthday was the next day I decided to spring a little extra cash on the B&B and take a zero for my birthday. What I learned that day was that the extra money was worth every penny. What made me happy was finding out that the B&B was perfectly located. It was right in the center of town on the main drag. The room was great; the shower wonderful, the owners were super-nice people and the breakfast was absolutely magnificent. The only breakfast I had on the trail that was better was at Mountain Harbour. Everything was made from scratch, prepared to order, and there was so much food I couldn't have possibly left hungry. It reminded me of breakfasts at B&B's in Scotland when I hiked the Great Glenn Way.

August 26th – My birthday and a zero day in Waynesboro, PA. I spoiled myself and had a great burger, fries and milkshake for lunch and a really fabulous birthday dinner at Sapporo Japanese Restaurant. The sashimi was as good as any I've ever eaten; the food was NYC-quality, a really awesome surprise for my 51st birthday. The most beautiful thing I saw that day was my sashimi plate, beet red, and fresh. The whole day made me happy; it was a really easy wonderful way to celebrate my birthday. What I learned that day wasn't really on my mind. I spent the day reflecting on the previous year. I'd started this whole crazy adventure to celebrate my 50th birthday and I was so happy and proud of the way the year had come off. I still had a lot in front of me; I would photograph Polar Bears for a week in Churchill on the Hudson Bay, and swim with Whale Sharks at the Georgia Aquarium. At the time that I'm writing this I've been on the road for thirteen months, and likely will stay on the road for another three or four months before fulling re-integrating into the default world. All of that was on my mind that wonderful day in Waynesboro, and it was one of the best birthdays I've ever had.

August 28th – This day was the very definition of a roller-coaster day and a validation of one of my favorite sayings, "It will all be fine in the end; if it's not fine, it's not the end." I was excited on the hike to hit the snack bar at the New Caledonia State Park; I was really craving a hot dog. I met a SOBO who had told me of a great barbecue place up the road from the park, but who had failed to mention that the snack bar in the park was closed. So, when I hit the edge of the park, I moved forward instead of heading towards the restaurant, only to find that the snack bar was closed. It was a major downer but I headed for the park headquarters knowing that at least they had a soda machine. I got to the machine and was so thrilled for a coke, but realized I didn't have singles. I went into park headquarters for change and, frankly, the woman working there acted like I didn't exist. Finally, a really nice older guy came over to me, asked me what I wanted, and gave me change. I went out to the soda machine and watched a guy buy a coke and was completely crushed to see the empty light go on; he'd bought the last one. I was so angry; if the woman hadn't ignored me for five minutes I'd be drinking a coke instead of standing there sweating my ass off. I settled for a Mountain Dew and went over and sat in the park to drink it.

I checked my phone for a signal and found a flaming email from a friend that ripped me up. The day was quickly diving down the rabbit hole. I tried unsuccessfully to Yogi in the park. It killed me to fail miserably, as I watched a number of families walking by with obviously not-fully-consumed containers of unnamed salads and snacks that, at that moment, I was convinced were the greatest tasting salads in the history of mankind. The only upside was the most beautiful thing I saw that day. A woman who was fully seven- or eight-months pregnant also had two munchkins, probably two-years and four-years old, in tow. They were really curious about me and started asking her questions and she said, go ask him. So the little four-year-old finally got up the courage to come over and ask me if I was a hiker. We had a great little conversation and I had both of them laughing; their laughs and smiles were definitely the most beautiful thing that day and had a great effect lifting my mood.

I lit out of the park and was moving up the trail quickly in the heat. It was one of those days where you are convinced you've hiked every bit of the distance to the shelter and more, and yet it is nowhere in sight. Then, you start getting paranoid, could I have missed the turn? At that point, every ten feet on the trail feels like a tenth of a mile, until that wonderful moment when you see the shelter. What I learned that day was to remember one of the core rules of hiking the Appalachian Trail: the trail provides. The shelter at Quarry Gap is the nicest shelter on the trail, and the caretaker was there. He was also the same guy who gave me change for the soda machine at the park headquarters. What made me happy was the half-hour conversation I had with him that day. He's a great guy, with a great perspective on the trail, and a long history of volunteering on it. His talk really made me feel great about being there and being on the trail in general. After I set up, I checked my phone and had a text from a beautiful woman, and an offer for a ride back home when I decided to finally come off the trail. A little while later, a Scottish girl I'd met the night before came into the shelter and we also had a great conversation. What had been a completely dreadful morning had turned into a really wonderful day. The trail provides.

August 29th – Holy shit it was hot! The heat and the humidity had been building for a couple of days and it was really hammering now. I stopped at Birch Run Shelter for a long lunch and a nap and saw the most beautiful thing for the day, as a couple of butterflies were flitting around and landed on my trekking poles. There is something really amazing to me about butterflies; they are so beautiful and fragile, sort of like blooming flowers that move around in the sky. Sitting there watching them was wonderful. After lunch I headed on to the shelter for the night; I got there relatively early and contemplated pushing into Pine Grove Furnace State Park and trying to hit the camp store and grill for dinner. But it was hot, and my Scottish friend was likely stopping at the same spot, so I decided to set up for the night. While I was setting up, a total trail character came through. Every now and then on the trail you meet people who can't be described any other way other than as a character. This guy was older, late 50's or a really-hard late 40's. He came up hiking with no shirt on, smoking a cigarette. His hair was just wild and his skin was so tanned and freckled that, at first, I didn't realize it wasn't a shirt. He was super-friendly, super-nice, and we had a great conversation for around fifteen minutes about absolutely nothing. As he was leaving, he mentioned his goal for the day; I told him it would be a big run, but he seemed unfazed at the prospect of another twenty miles that day and I'd love to know if he made it.

My Scottish friend came in a little while later and we hung our hammocks down near the stream. It was a great little spot with a picnic table, and we made dinner and settled in for the night. She would teach me about Time Lord Rock that night. Being a Doctor Who fan, I was really excited to learn about this. She played me a couple of songs off her phone and it was amazing. She also hiked with a ukulele and was quite talented. As I settled into sleep, she was playing; she started to put it away and I told her to feel free to keep playing. I fell asleep that night to the sweet sounds of her playing. She was really talented and it was one of the most amazing moments on the trail for me. Unfortunately, I never heard from her after we parted ways the next day, but she was a great hiking partner.

August 30th – My Scottish friend and I had talked a lot the night before about the next morning's breakfast at the camp store and grill in Pine Grove Furnace State Park. I was heavily fixated on the idea of a bacon and egg sandwich, and had warned my partner I'd likely be up and out early to be at the store when it opened. I didn't quite make it out that early, but the most beautiful thing I saw that day was that bacon and egg sandwich; it was large and wonderful on a gorgeous hard roll. I wolfed that sandwich down in two minutes and ordered a second. It was early and it was already getting hot. My hiking partner came in about an hour later and ordered breakfast while I had my third. The store is the home of the half-gallon ice cream challenge. Thru-hikers stop there to see how fast they can eat a half-gallon of ice cream. I passed on the opportunity, but not on lunch; my fourth meal of the day there. The heat and humidity were brutal and my friend looked at me and said, "I'm not sure I'm hiking anymore today." I knew I wasn't and as I sat there, looking at the weather forecast for the next few days (more heat and humidity) I knew I was finally done. I had passed the thousand-mile mark that morning coming into Pine Grove, and it hit me in that moment that not only was I done for the day, I was done with the trail. I'd made my goal. My total tally was 1002 miles. I was happy and it was a wonderful day. I decided to go out on a good note and went and got a milkshake. I informed my friend of my decision and then treated us to a campsite in the park for the night.

Fittingly, the night would be filled with heavy rain and thunderstorms, but before they started we got showers and set up. What I learned that day was that parting wasn't always sad; my friend would move on in the morning while I got a ride to the train station. What had made me happy that day was simply hiking a thousand miles on the Appalachian Trail. A feat that, to some, sounds unbelievable. And yet I was feeling a little inadequate compared to friends who were even then pushing through Maine, to Katahdin. I felt inadequate but satisfied; I was envious of my friends' accomplishments, but more than satisfied with my own.

CHAPTER EIGHT

Reflections

Coming to the end of my Appalachian Trail journey sent millions of thoughts through my head. The first thing I reflected on was what it meant to quit the Appalachian Trail now that I was finally and officially abandoning it.

Once you're on the trail, you realize some things quickly; it's amazing out there and doing the AT is really hard. You expect that the weight will be an issue, as well as the terrain and the weather, but there really is no way to truly simulate the mental and physical work of a long distance thru-hike . . . without doing a thru-hike. As such, you see people with many levels of physical and mental preparedness for the adventure. And although people quit for a lot of reasons, a lack of physical and/or mental preparation is a big one. Because you truly can't be completely ready for your first thru-hike attempt. It's important to be as prepared as possible; going out there completely unprepared is usually a recipe for disaster. But I say "usually" because you will always run into someone who will tell you about their sister's husband's brother's friend who had never hiked before and came out totally unprepared and completed the whole trail. I'm sure it has happened.

Some quit because they have to; injury, illness, life's responsibilities—all can end a thru-hike. Some decide that they like the *idea* of being a thru-hiker but don't enjoy thru-hiking, and no one should do something so hard if they don't enjoy it. I was on the trail long enough to watch a number of people whom I knew and liked, quit their hike. Their decisions were agony!

When you finally decide to quit the trail, you feel like you have failed (at first). This idea is ridiculous; by even attempting a thru-hike you have been more adventurous than 90% of the people you know. Starting a thru-hike means you took a risk. Many of us quit jobs, sold houses, etc., to go do it. These are not small things, and, by themselves, these actions change your life.

Second, you feel like you have let people down. You have told everyone you're going to do it. Many of us had social media followings. So, when you quit, you feel like you have let all of those people down. Happily, most people are really supportive of the decision you made, understanding the immensity of the task and that you didn't make the decision to quit lightly. Inevitably, some jerk is going to beat you up verbally for quitting and not completing the hike to Maine. My reply to them: if you did more miles on the AT than the person you're beating-on, then you have some right to your opinion. If you haven't, you need to shut-the-hell-up, because you don't understand, nor have you accomplished what that person has done. I do have to say, to this point I haven't encountered anyone who has given me a hard time about quitting. In general, people do seem to get the immensity of even attempting a thru-hike.

Finally, quitting brings up the inevitable question of, "what now?" You've changed your life and planned for six months on the trail; often to use the time to work out what's next. Suddenly that decision is very, very imminent and that can be terrifying.

I hope this helps people understand this a bit. Some of the folks I know who have left the trail struggled with the decision they needed to make for themselves. Most of them are now happily doing well. I have immense respect for anyone who attempts to complete this journey, no matter how many steps they take on the trail. It is about the process, the journey, and the transformative nature of the experience, not the number of miles completed. We should celebrate and support these magnificent risk-takers for what they attempted and accomplished, not make them feel bad for what anyone else thinks they should have done. I think it's important that at all times we try to be kind, supportive and empathetic of what others are trying to accomplish in life, no matter what it is. I also want to point out that because it is such a difficult task, I have much respect for people who walked all 2189 miles. They are absolutely amazing humans.

The journey of a thousand miles starts with one step – **Lao Tzu**

Given my thousand miles on the trail, this quote really hits home for me and leads to my first really special moment on the trail. Several years ago, at a sustainability workshop in Vermont, I met some great folks. Several of them have become friends, and one, Jim Cooper, currently lives in Georgia. Jim offered to hike me into the AT at Amicalola State Falls Park. We met up at the Hike Inn and spent the night there, and the next day Jim walked me to the junction-point between the Approach Trail and his trail back out of the park. It was really special having a friend come along on the starting part of my journey.

The bond that links your true family is not one of blood, but of respect and joy in each other's life. ~ **Richard Bach**

I've written about the importance of trail community on the AT. But an important subset of the overall community is your trail family. The quote above applies every bit as much to my trail family as any blood family. I had a lot of hiking partners on the trail, but some of the folks I spent the most time with have truly become family. My trail family was first born on the climb outside of the Nantahala Outdoor Center. That day, four old bastards engaged in what felt like a straight up, never-ending hike. It was a warm day and water wasn't as plentiful as we had hoped. We were worn-out on the climb, but we were also smiling and laughing. There was a sudden search for some really fragrant flowers that turned out to be Backtrack's bug spray; and Awesome, who was damn near out of water, suddenly disappeared up the trail like a miner chasing gold nuggets, when he heard there was water ahead.

We reached the top of the climb and we were whooped but happy. Although a couple of us would move further down the trail, that day would cement the first incarnation of what came to be known as the AARP Gang, the name coming from the fact that the youngest member of our group was 49.

The AARP Gang would expand over time and would include the four original members, Second Star, and the one full-completer in the group, Jedi. At times we also had some other wonderful hikers with us: Mad Hatter, Appendicitis (tough cookie), and Optimist, and others. My apologies to anyone I've failed to mention.

Just as we develop our physical muscles through overcoming opposition – such as lifting weights – we develop our character muscles by overcoming challenges and adversity ~ **Stephen Covey**

Hiking the Appalachian Trail is an amazing thing, primarily because of the hiking community that you encounter. I encounter the same sort of thing at the Burning Man Festival that I have attended a number of times.

At Burning Man you meet an incredible group of people. People are kinder than the folks you normally encounter; they are giving, open people who have a similar mindset to you in many ways. The normal stresses of life are put on hold and you get to relax in a way you never get to do in your day-to-day, default life. One of the things that you notice just after Burning Man is people leave the desert, hit the tarmac and revert to the same behaviors they normally exhibit off the playa. And it begins to bum you out. Then, once you get back to the default world you quickly remember why your time at Burning Man (like your time on the trail) was so special. You quickly get disillusioned with society and the people you encounter. You long for the community you left behind, and it leads, in the case of Burning Man, to what I call Post Playa Depression.

Once you're off the trail, you'll feel some of these same feelings. We miss our trail family. Life becomes more complex and not nearly as satisfying as life on the trail. Being on the trail we had clear, defined, and simple goals – hike to that point from this point. We feel bummed-out by the complexity of the default world, so what do we do?

The very first thing I would say is: be careful with any big decisions you have decided to make. If it's something you've been thinking about for months on the trail, you're probably ok. But if it's a sudden decision you're making—one you haven't been considering on the trail—be careful; take your time before acting and make sure it's a good decision and not one born out of your longing for the connections you're missing.

Stay connected. Your trail family is still out there and they're feeling the same way you are, so reach out. Give them a call, drop them a note, plan a hike somewhere with one or all of them. Write about your experiences—in a book, a blog, or even just in your own journal. Remind yourself of all of the positive things you have just experienced. Then, start planning your next adventure; you've just done something completely out of the box and utterly amazing. What's next for you? The possibilities are endless and now you know that you are capable of doing something amazing.

Stay in shape; don't underestimate the positive impacts of the daily exercise regime you've been implementing for the last few months. Sure, you aren't going to replicate walking eight-plus hours a day with weight on your back, but you can stay active by walking, biking, running, or going to the gym. Keep exercising daily; exercise will not only keep you fit and help keep off post-trail weight, but regular exercise has an impact on your mood. Likewise, get off your trail diet and back to eating less. Make sure it's more balanced and healthier food.

Finally, stay happy. Do the basic things we know help make people happier. Exercise, express gratitude, get enough sleep, smile, be altruistic, show off your pictures, and tell people about what you just did. People love hearing about the trail; they love to live vicariously through our experiences. It will make you feel good and likely get you more than a couple of free drinks.

Also, feel free to reach out to the hiking community, which includes me. Find someone to talk to if you are feeling down. And I mean this my friends. If you need to talk, I'm here, and so are your fellow brothers and sisters from the hiking community. We were there for each other on the trail and we can be here for each other off the trail.

Changes

The first step toward change is awareness, the second is acceptance.
~ **Nathaniel Branden**

When I first started this hike, people continually asked me why I would attempt a thru-hike of the Appalachian Trail. The answer I have settled on is: *Hiking the Appalachian Trail is an adventure and adventure leads to transformation and I want to lead a transformational life.* That, of course, means embracing change, something I am really weird about because I'm one of the few of us who actually likes change. I think it comes from getting bored easily.

However, that does not mean that change doesn't scare the hell out of me, like it does everyone else. What it does mean is that I'm willing to push through the fear and take the leap. For me, the only really hard part is the first step; once I've started, my fear is gone. So, what really holds most of us back is not our circumstances, but the doubts and fears within our own heads. I'm here to say you *can* take that first step and do amazing things other people don't do.

One of the changes I have experienced after my first couple of months on the trail didn't become apparent to me for some time. I had developed a deep affection for the mountains. I've always been an outdoorsman; my whole life I have hiked, hunted, photographed and fished. Being in the woods in the fall has always been a precious thing to me. But being off the trail I actually find myself longing to be back out there; in many ways it has become home. I've said on several occasions while on the trail that I didn't know if the experience would lead me to spending more time in the woods, or if I'd never go hiking again. I can say for a fact it will be the former not the latter.

First you examine your surroundings, then you examine your gear, then you examine yourself ~ **Colin Fletcher**

This quote by Colin Fletcher is perhaps my favorite quote about hiking. It's also one of the most accurate. You go through phases on a long hike. First, there is the amazement of your surroundings: the forest, the flowers, the views, the difficulty or ease of the topography. Then, when the initial wonderment wears off, you start analyzing how well your gear is functioning, how much weight can I drop out of my pack, why the hell did I bring three lighters when I have a self-igniting stove?

Finally, when you can no longer avoid it, particularly when the trail is difficult and you have to be focused and mindful of your steps, you get into your own head. Humans have two superpowers in my opinion: the abilities to rationalize and deny anything. We use these skills to avoid thinking about life's bigger questions. However, after some time in the woods, you can no longer escape yourself. You come face-to-face with all of the questions you avoid on a daily basis. Some are universal, some incredibly unique and personal. The process is less about "finding" yourself and more about revealing the true you that has been lying underneath layers of societally required masks and personal bullshit.

I'm fortunate, I've been hacking away at those layers for some time, so getting to the real me hasn't been that hard. The hard part is, now that I'm there, what the hell do I do? I think my plan is intact, it's time to take some risks and try and live the life I envision instead of the one that was safest and made the most sense. At 52, perhaps I'm getting here really late, perhaps I'm early to the party, we'll see.

Learning Acceptance

My happiness grows in direct proportion to my acceptance and in inverse proportion to my expectations ~ **Michael J Fox**

When you set out to do a long-distance thru-hike on the Appalachian Trail you know a few things in advance. You know it will be hard and you know you will be dirty and wet and smelly. You know you'll likely lose some weight. You also know that that you will go through some form of transformation; you'll change in some way, maybe many ways. One of the things that hit me while hiking in Vermont and Massachusetts was that the trail teaches you acceptance.

You see, when you are out on the trail, life is simplified to the basics: food, shelter, the weather. The simple fact is that many of the things you deal with each day are completely out of your control. On the trail you have to accept the topography. Whether you will climb big hills, do sharp descents, walk over rocks and in mud, or on heavenly flat trails, you just have to walk. I've taken to not asking about the trail ahead to hikers I pass going the other way. It doesn't matter. I know the profile and the distances from the guide I carry; whether it will be hard or easy is a matter of opinion. No matter what the trail holds, we're going to walk it. So what's coming really starts to not matter; it's just another hill, man. You have to accept the trail for what it is, and even more importantly, find happiness in not only smooth descents, but in the hard climbs and the rocky trails. If you can't get to this point, the trail can be a very hard place indeed. And in the end, this is an absolutely perfect metaphor being happy in life.

The other big thing on the trail that you have no control over is the weather. We all know that we will get rained on while we are on the trail. However, sometimes it can be a bit daunting. Starting the trail in early March it rained, sleeted or snowed 12 out of the first 14 days on the trail. It was a bit much, it almost broke me; I hadn't quite gotten to the point of acceptance yet. During my week on the trail in Vermont we got wet, and basically stayed damp for the rest of the week. When it rains a lot the humidity stays up, your gear stays wet, and it's unpleasant. But it is what it is, and you will have weeks like this on the trail, so you just have to come to accept it.

Acceptance doesn't mean you don't take precautions; I blue blazed Albert Mountain in bad weather because of a bad knee and my poor descending skills. I've stayed an extra day in town or delayed returning to the trail to miss a day of bad weather. But once on the trail I accept what's coming, this attitude has made being on the trail a much happier experience. Being wet, tired, smelly, climbing big hills and hard terrain is all part of doing a thru-hike, and with that acceptance comes a level of happiness that sustains you on the trail.

The real trick in life is to find ways to take that level of acceptance and transfer it to life in the default world. Can you learn to accept that you'll be cut off in traffic, that pipes will break, that the cable will go out, and that the package that you paid extra to have arrive on Friday isn't coming until Monday? If you can, maybe, just maybe, we can be as happy in our default world lives as a thru-hiker on the Appalachian Trail.

Reflections on life and happiness at the end of a journey

Never too old, never too bad, never too late, never too sick to start from scratch once again ~ **Bikram Choudhury**

Some people think a life where you follow your bliss is not as valid or valuable as a life that follows society's script. I disagree, and the evidence I present are the hikers I met every day on the trail. They were some of the happiest people I've ever met and every one of them was off of society's script. I return to something I'd heard pre-hike, and that I can attest to from my own experience: 90% of the hikers I met were happy 90% of the time. You don't see that level of happiness anywhere in the default world.

I started the Ministry of Happiness Blog in 2010.The purpose was to help me explore the idea of happiness after years of fighting depression, and to hopefully pass this information on to help others live a happier life. I've come to believe that the best way to happiness is through adventure. Whether those adventures are small or large is irrelevant, what's important is the effort—that you stretch yourself and change the conditions that leave you less happy than you want to be in your life. Adventure leads to new and wonderful experiences, and it has been shown that buying experiences instead of things makes you happier. So, taking on the Appalachian Trail is the sort of adventure that leads, as I hope the preceding pages have shown, to magnificent experiences both large and small.

If this book provides you nothing but a smile, and some fun reading, then, fantastic! But there is also a message in this story that I hope you get. It's a message that I relay often and one that I hope you will take to heart: ***Yes you can!*** Not an original message, it's a little tweak on Cesar Chavez's Si se puede, which was then translated and used by the Obama campaign in the form you most likely know: "Yes, we can." But this is a personal message, so it's yes *you* can, and *you can*. I know you can my friends, whatever it is; the only thing that stops us is not trying. If this fifty-something, lazy fat man can jump out on the Appalachian Trail and walk a thousand miles you can do anything you set your mind to do. Sure, it may be very hard. Yes, there will be obstacles to starting and completing. The complexity and responsibilities in our life may make it seem impossible. It may take a long time and it will take planning. But all of those things can be dealt with if you want it enough and are willing to just take that first step. It's always the hardest one. I will come back to Lao Tzu one last time, my journey of a thousand miles started with just one step and yours can, too. Yes you can, my friends, and you'll be happier for it. I know I am.

~ Michael "Reverend" Kane

ABOUT THE AUTHOR

Michael "Rev" Kane is the creator of the Ministry of Happiness blog
(https://RevKane.com). He is a writer, educator, photographer, adventurer
and general sampler of life. He has spent time trekking in the Himalayas,
cycling in Ireland, walking the Great Glen Way in Scotland, photographing
polar bears, swimming with whale sharks and of course hiking over a
thousand miles on the Appalachian Trail. Most recently he visited Petra
and Wadi Rum in the Jordan desert and floated on his back for the first
time ever in the Dead Sea. He has a simple philosophy, adventure leads to
a happier life. He believes, adventure come in many sizes and it's never too
late to find your adventure and have happy days!

40106039R00064

Made in the USA
Middletown, DE
03 February 2017